J. D. SALINGER

Modern Critical Views

These and other titles in preparation

Modern Critical Views

J. D. SALINGER

Edited and with an introduction by
Harold Bloom
Sterling Professor of the Humanities
Yale University

CHELSEA HOUSE PUBLISHERS ◇ 1987
New York ◇ New Haven ◇ Philadelphia

© 1987 by Chelsea House Publishers, a division of Chelsea House Educational Communications, Inc.,
  95 Madison Avenue, New York, NY 10016
  345 Whitney Avenue, New Haven, CT 06511
  5014 West Chester Pike, Edgemont, PA 19028

Introduction © 1987 by Harold Bloom

Printed and bound in the United States of America

∞ The paper used in this publication meets the minimum requirements of the American National Standard for Permanence of Paper for Printed Library Materials, Z39.48-1984.

Library of Congress Cataloging-in-Publication Data
J. D. Salinger.
    (Modern critical views)
    Bibliography: p.
    Includes index.
    Contents: J. D. Salinger, Seventy eight bananas / William Wiegand—J. D. Salinger, everybody's favorite / Alfred Kazin—The love ethic / David D. Galloway—[etc.]
    1. Salinger, J. D. (Jerome David), 1919–   —Criticism and interpretation. [1. Salinger, J. D. (Jerome David), 1919–   —Criticism and interpretations.   2. American literature—Criticism and interpretations]   I. Bloom, Harold.   II. Series.
PS3537.A426Z67   1987   813′.54   86-29941
ISBN 0-87754-716-5 (alk. paper)

Contents

Editor's Note

This book gathers together what I judge to be the best criticism available upon the fiction of J. D. Salinger. The critical essays are reprinted here in the chronological order of their original publication. I am grateful to David Parker for his work as a researcher upon this volume.

My introduction attempts an estimate of *The Catcher in the Rye* as a kind of Gatsby-like, modern version of Twain's *Huckleberry Finn*. William Wiegand begins the chronological sequence of criticism with a reading of Salinger's one novel and some of the subsequent stories that depict the hero as drifting in the currents of his own psyche, fleeing nothing in particular, and seeking nothing in particular. *Franny and Zooey* is analyzed by Alfred Kazin, who finds Salinger to be marked by a perpetual and self-indulgent immaturity.

Salinger's love ethic is seen by David D. Galloway as a rejection of mysticism, but only through the affirmation of the absurdist love incarnated in Seymour, who dies so that Franny and Zooey may live. Max F. Schulz, meditating upon "Seymour: An Introduction," finds in it a crisis of consciousness that Salinger's recourse to Zen Buddhism cannot resolve. Holden and Seymour, considered together by Helen Weinberg, are seen as types of spiritual hero, and rather dangerously are compared to Kafka's protagonists.

Zen, which seems to me Salinger's most inauthentic resource, is applied to *Nine Stories* by Bernice and Sanford Goldstein, who find in it his serious principle of integration. Gerald Rosen, retrospectively gazing at *The Catcher in the Rye*, takes Zen more casually as a reinforcement of Salinger's conviction that each of us must work out his or her own mode of salvation.

In an analysis of "For Esmé—with Love and Squalor," John Wenke discovers in the story the seeds of Salinger's stance of silence. Dennis L. O'Connor concludes this book by presenting "Raise High the Roof Beam, Carpenters" as an example of what he believes to be Salinger's religious pluralism, and which he relates to the long and honorable American literary tradition of Transcendentalism that began with Emerson and his greatest disciples, Thoreau and Whitman.

Introduction

I

The Salinger legend, both powerful and colorless, almost more powerful for the lack of color, seems less important now, in 1986, after twenty years of silence on the writer's part. *The Catcher in the Rye* (1951); *Nine Stories* (1953); *Franny and Zooey* (1961); *Raise High the Roof Beam, Carpenters* and *Seymour: An Introduction* (1963) —these constitute Salinger's saga. Perhaps Salinger outlived his gift; perhaps something more eventually will be published. There is a curious completeness in his four short books, taken together. The first two are minor masterpieces or minor classics, and remind us that "minor" can be a descriptive as well as an evaluative word in literary criticism.

Despite his personal relationship with Hemingway, Salinger derives from Scott Fitzgerald. Holden Caulfield and Seymour Glass are clearly in the visionary mode of Jay Gatsby, and Holden's first-person narrative owes more to Nick Carraway than to Huck Finn. A comparison to Fitzgerald is dangerous for Salinger. *The Catcher in the Rye* is hardly of *The Great Gatsby*'s aesthetic dignity, nor will "A Perfect Day for Bananafish" quite survive side-by-side reading with "Babylon Revisited." This is not to deprecate Salinger but to indicate his limits; his narrative art is shadowed by Fitzgerald's.

A lack of originality is not likely to dim Salinger's permanent appeal to perpetually fresh generations of young readers. Rereading Salinger is, however, partly spoiled by his felt lack of exuberance in characterization or spontaneity through narrative invention. What once seemed original about Salinger, his Zen spirituality, now is revealed as a mere fashion of middlebrow culture in the United States of the fifties and early sixties. Seymour Glass as Zen saint is hardly a persuasive fictive representation in the United States of the middle eighties.

The Glass family saga is a collection of period pieces, like the *Rabbit* novels of John Updike, or Walker Percy's neo-Catholic, polemical fictions that have

1

followed *The Moviegoer*. *The Catcher in the Rye* seems much more than that, as are a few of the *Nine Stories*. Period pieces, when well-wrought, eventually can acquire an antique charm, but first they go through an ambiguous phase where they are merely quaint. Salinger's skills as a writer are admirable, perhaps too overtly admirable, in the manner of the *New Yorker*, with its period styles. Scott Fitzgerald touched his own kind of American Sublime by bringing together a Conradian moral intensity with a legitimate prose version of a Keatsian lyricism. We derive an easier pleasure through reading Salinger, who cannot persuade us that he can substitute the experience of reading him for more difficult and demanding literary pleasures.

II

The pleasures of *The Catcher in the Rye* adequately are revealed by its famous first paragraph:

If you really want to hear about it, the first thing you'll probably want to know is where I was born, and what my lousy childhood was like, and how my parents were occupied and all before they had me, and all that David Copperfield kind of crap, but I don't feel like going into it, if you want to know the truth. In the first place, that stuff bores me, and in the second place, my parents would have about two hemorrhages apiece if I told anything pretty personal about them. They're quite touchy about anything like that, especially my father. They're *nice* and all—I'm not saying that—but they're also touchy as hell. Besides, I'm not going to tell you my whole goddam autobiography or anything. I'll just tell you about this madman stuff that happened to me around last Christmas just before I got pretty run-down and had to come out here and take it easy. I mean that's all I told D.B. about, and he's my *brother* and all. He's in Hollywood. That isn't too far from this crumby place, and he comes over and visits me practically every week end. He's going to drive me home when I go home next month maybe. He just got a Jaguar. One of those little English jobs that can do around two hundred miles an hour. It cost him damn near four thousand bucks. He's got a lot of dough, now. He didn't *use* to. He used to be just a regular writer, when he was home. He wrote this terrific book of short stories, *The Secret Goldfish*, in case you never heard of him. The best one in it was "The Secret Goldfish." It was about this little kid that wouldn't let anybody look at his goldfish because he'd

bought it with his own money. It killed me. Now he's out in Hollywood, D.B., being a prostitute. If there's one thing I hate, it's the
movies. Don't even mention them to me.

The ear, inner and outer, is certainly evident, and the tone is alive and
consistent. What we miss, as we age into rereaders, is surprise, even when Holden
signs off with some grace:

D.B. asked me what I thought about all this stuff I just finished
telling you about. I didn't know what the hell to say. If you want to
know the truth, I don't *know* what I think about it. I'm sorry I told
so many people about it. About all I know is, I sort of *miss* everybody I told about. Even old Stradlater and Ackley, for instance. I
think I even miss that goddam Maurice. It's funny. Don't ever tell
anybody anything. If you do, you start missing everybody.

One thinks of Huck Finn's evenhanded mode of narration, with its constant undersong of fellow-feeling and compassion, and of Nick Carraway's fair-
mindedness, and even of Jake Barnes's rueful affection for almost anyone whose
story he has told. Holden Caulfield has added a certain zany zest, but little else.
Yet that is to grant Salinger's best book rather less than it merits, since no book
can touch the universal, even for a time, without a gift of its own for the
receptive reader.

Holden is derivative, but still highly likeable, and for all his vulnerability he
remains an attractive survivor, who has returned from illness as his narrative
ends. Survival is his entire enterprise, even as freedom was Huck Finn's enterprise. This regression from freedom to survival is what gives Salinger's one novel
its curious pathos, which is also its principal aesthetic virtue. Endlessly honest
with the reader, Holden wistfully keeps revealing that his outcast condition is
only partly a voluntary one. He is potentially self-destructive, very nearly maso-
chistic in his psychosexuality, and religiously obsessed, to the extent that he
admires poor Legion, the madman and tomb-haunter, trapped by many demons.
The most unpleasant sentence in the novel is surely Holden's declaration: "If you
want to know the truth, the guy I like best in the Bible, next to Jesus, was that
lunatic and all, that lived in the tombs."

Any aesthetic judgment of *The Catcher in the Rye* turns finally upon its
most famous passage, which is what might be called its title-passage:

I'm not too sure old Phoebe knew what the hell I was talking about.
I mean she's only a little child and all. But she was listening, at least.
If somebody at least listens, it's not too bad.
    "Daddy's going to kill you. He's going to *kill* you," she said.

I wasn't listening, though. I was thinking about something else—something crazy. "You know what I'd like to be?" I said. "You know what I'd like to be? I mean if I had my goddam choice?"

"What? Stop *swear*ing."

"You know that song 'If a body catch a body comin' through the rye'? I'd like—"

"It's 'If a body *meet* a body coming through the rye'!" old Phoebe said. "It's a poem. By Robert *Burns*."

"I *know* it's a poem by Robert Burns."

She was right, though. It *is* "If a body meet a body coming through the rye." I didn't know it then, though.

"I thought it was 'If a body catch a body,' " I said. "Anyway, I keep picturing all these little kids playing some game in this big field of rye and all. Thousands of little kids, and nobody's around—nobody big, I mean—except me. And I'm standing on the edge of some crazy cliff. What I have to do, I have to catch everybody if they start to go over the cliff—I mean if they're running and they don't look where they're going I have to come out from somewhere and *catch* them. That's all I'd do all day. I'd just be the catcher in the rye and all. I know it's crazy, but that's the only thing I'd really like to be. I know it's crazy."

Old Phoebe didn't say anything for a long time. Then, when she said something, all she said was, "Daddy's going to kill you."

From "meet" to "catch" is Holden's revision, and Salinger's vital epiphany, as it were. Huck Finn's story, on this basis, might have been called *The Meeter in the Rye*. To meet is to be free; to catch is to aid survival, and somehow to survive.

WILLIAM WIEGAND

J. D. Salinger:
Seventy-Eight Bananas

Six years have passed since the publication of J. D. Salinger's single novel, *The Catcher in the Rye*, yet the author still retains his transfixing influence on the very young writer. The guileless "It killed me; it really did" idiom has captured hundreds of imitators during this time; and the imprint of Salinger's hero, Holden Caulfield, the boy who left fencing foils on the subway and wound up on a psychiatrist's couch, has engrafted itself so indelibly on the separate imaginations that young heroes by the scores have been spawned in his image.

Yet Salinger remains undignified by any very close attention to his work. On one hand, he has been regarded as innocuously sentimental (John Aldridge says so); on the other, he has been found insufferably crude (one large western university, for example, fired an instructor for using *The Catcher in the Rye* in a freshman literature class). Still, he has not been conscientiously rejected so much as he has been righteously ignored.

This neglect is unfortunate for at least two reasons. First of all, and perhaps less important, Salinger has, in a measure, revived the dormant art of dialect in American fiction. His ear has detected innumerable idiomatic expressions that were simply unrecorded before. And with this gift he has been able to reach a level of readers that Mark Twain, for example, was able to reach. Unlike others who have made the attempt to transcribe distinctive speech patterns, Salinger has succeeded, as few beyond Twain have, in making his characters something more than cracker-barrel philosophers or, worse, good-natured boobs.

But this achievement is somewhat self-evident. I prefer to justify Salinger on a second basis: namely, the coherence of his particular vision of the world.

From *The Chicago Review* 11, no. 4 (Winter 1958). © 1958 by the *Chicago Review*.

This is essentially the vision of his heroes—of Holden Caulfield, Seymour Glass, Teddy, Franny, Daumier-Smith, and the rest. The important question in Salinger is why these intelligent, highly sensitive, affectionate beings fight curious, gruelling battles, leaderless and causeless, in a world they never made.

In simple terms, they are a family of nonconformists and Salinger documents their brotherhood by presenting several of them as brothers and sisters in "Franny," "Raise High the Roof Beam, Carpenters," and "Zooey," his most recent stories. However, this is not traditional nonconformity. Logically, the enemy of the nonconformist is society or some oppressive segment of society; and in the recent tradition from Sinclair Lewis's Arrowsmith and Hemingway's Frederick Henry right down to Ayn Rand's Howard Roark, the nonconformist hero is constantly threatened by external forces which seek to inhibit and to destroy him. With the Salinger hero, however, the conflict is never so cleanly drawn. Holden does not leave the fencing team's foils on the subway because of any direct external pressure, nor does he flunk out of Pencey and the other schools because of unreasonable demands made on him. Holden knows this as well as anybody. He is a victim not so much of society as of his own spiritual illness.

Salinger has spent much of his career seeking a cure for this illness; however, before we examine that search, we need a somewhat more precise definition of the illness. Perhaps it is best described in his second to last story "Raise High the Roof Beam, Carpenters," a work which amplifies and explains the first of the Nine Stories, "A Perfect Day for Bananafish." The earlier story describes the last few hours in the life of Seymour Glass and is a brief, impersonally told, and slightly obscure work. The later story, seven or eight times as long, tells of Seymour's wedding day some years before his death. Its main scene is a long interlude in a taxicab in which Seymour is discussed by several interested parties, including his brother Buddy. It concludes with sections from Seymour's personal journal, material designed to explain why he leaves his bride at the altar, and to suggest why he kills himself after several years of marriage. Without "Carpenters" the suicide which closes "Bananafish" appears motivated chiefly by Seymour's inability to put up with his bourgeois wife. With "Carpenters," however, we see Seymour as a man not deprived of, but rather surfeited with, the joy of life. Salinger's sole excuse for Seymour's desperate social irresponsibility is this same curious surfeit of sensation.

We learn, for example, in the course of "Carpenters," that Seymour does not show up for his wedding because he is too "happy," or as he puts it in his journal, he is "too keyed up . . . to be with people." The nature of this happiness is further illuminated through the use of a boyhood experience of Seymour's: at the age of twelve he threw a stone at a young girl, scarring her for life. Seymour's brother, the narrator, explains the incident this way:

We were up at the Lake. Seymour had written to Charlotte, inviting her to come and visit us, and her mother finally let her. What happened was, she sat down in the middle of our driveway one morning to pet Boo Boo's cat, and Seymour threw a stone at her. He was twelve. That's all there was to it. He threw it at her because she looked so beautiful sitting there in the middle of the driveway with Boo Boo's cat. Everybody knew that, for God's sake—me, Charlotte, Boo Boo, Waker, Walt, the whole family.

Seymour's own understanding of his malady is a more poetic one. He writes in his journal:

If or when I do start going to an analyst, I hope to God he has the foresight to let a dermatologist sit in on the consultation. A hand specialist. I have scars on my hands from touching certain people. Once, in the park, when Franny was still in the carriage, I put my hand on the downy pate of her head and left it there too long. Another time, at Loew's Seventy-second Street, with Zooey during a spooky movie. He was about six or seven, and he went under the seat to avoid watching a scary scene. I put my hand on his head. Certain heads, certain colors and textures of human hair leave permanent marks on me. Other things too. Charlotte once ran away from me outside the studio, and I grabbed her dress to stop her, to keep her near me. A yellow cotton dress I loved because it was too long for her. I still have a lemon-yellow mark on the palm of my right hand. Oh, God, if I'm anything by a clinical name, I'm a kind of paranoiac in reverse. I suspect people of plotting to make me happy.

The "skin disease" which Seymour sees himself afflicted with in 1942 apparently becomes worse. By 1948, the date of his suicide, the "lemon-yellow marks" have attained weight and shape; he has become mortally ill.

During the course of his interlude with the little girl on the beach in "A Perfect Day for Bananafish," he says to her:

"You just keep your eyes open for any bananafish. This is a perfect day for bananafish."

"I don't see any," Sybil said.

"That's understandable. Their habits are very peculiar. . . . They lead a very tragic life. . . . You know what they do, Sybil?"

She shook her head.

"Well, they swim into a hole where there's a lot of bananas. They're very ordinary-looking fish when they swim *in*. But once they

get in, they behave like pigs. Why I've known some bananafish to
swim into a banana hole and eat as many as seventy-eight bananas.
. . . Naturally after that they're so fat they can't get out of the hole
again. Can't fit through the door."
   . . . "What happens to them?"
   . . . "Well, I hate to tell you, Sybil. They die."
"Why?" asked Sybil.
"Well, they get banana fever. It's a terrible disease."

In other words, Seymour, a bananafish himself, has become so glutted with
sensation that he cannot swim out into society again. It is his own banana fever,
not his wife who is at fault, or his mother-in-law. If they are stupid and insensitive, "Carpenters" shows them also to be without malice, and hence basically as
inculpable for the bananafish's condition as is the Matron of Honor, who represents the whole levelheaded society in criticizing Seymour for his peccadilloes.

In general, the bananafish diagnosis applies to all the Salinger invalids.
Holden Caulfield's trouble, for example, is not that he hates, or that he fears, or,
as Aldridge suggests, that he has no goals—but rather that he has no capacity to
purge his sensations. He is blown up like a balloon, or like a bananafish, with his
memories. He says at the very end of the novel: "About all I know is, I sort of
miss everybody I told about. Even old Stradlater and Ackley, for instance. I think
I even miss that goddam Maurice. It's funny." Thus, with the good things he
remembers like Allie, his dead brother, and like Jane, the girl who kept her kings
in the back row, he retains the bad things as well—until nothing is either good
or bad after a point, but simply retained and cherished as a part of himself,
submerging him with the sheer weight of the accumulated burden.

The important word in the passage quoted above is "miss." What is un-
bearable is not that some people are bad, but that experience is fleeting. Everything must be retained. The image Holden has for himself of being "the catcher
in the rye" is the perfect metaphor for this objective. He wants to guard the
children from falling off the edge of the rye field; likewise he tries to guard each
experience from falling into oblivion. With this perspective he fails to discriminate between "important" and "unimportant" experiences to determine which
to retain and which to reject—and the bananafish becomes the more bloated
and uncomfortable. The "perfect day" is the day when the bananafish is able to
end all his suffering by killing himself.

                                    II

In going back, we find the bananafish in embryo even in Salinger's very
early stories. Most of those which appeared in the *Saturday Evening Post* and

Collier's during the war years are rather standard pieces about GIs which the magazines were full of then. But what is distinctive about them perhaps is a particular undertone of very imminent tragedy: the moment imperiled by what is to come. Even the glimpses of life we get away from the front are fraught with a fragile sense of impermanence. Everything is in a state of flux. There is no arrested moment.

The hero of three of these stories is John (Babe) Gladwaller. For the most part, Babe is a Hemingway soldier who suffers in silence. Occasionally, however, there are clues of self-torment in the character, traits which are to become the hallmark of the Salinger heroes in the late stories. In "The Last Day of the Last Furlough," Babe speaks of a girl he loves. "The more unrequited my love for her becomes," (he says), "the longer I love her, the oftener I whip out my dumb heart like crazy X-Ray pictures, the greater the urge to trace the bruises."

"The Stranger" closes with Babe's little sister jumping off the curb into the street as Babe walks beside her. "Why was it such a beautiful thing to see?" he asks, as if with an urge to fight the feeling for its very largeness. In *Catcher*, the same situation is echoed in Phoebe's carousel ride. Holden says of it, "I felt so damn happy all of a sudden, the way old Phoebe kept going around and around. I was damn near bawling. I felt so damn happy, if you want to know the truth. I don't know why. It was just that she looked so damn *nice*, the way she kept going around and around, in her blue coat and all. God, I wish you could've been there."

The Babe Gladwaller stories therefore foreshadow what is to become the chief concern in Salinger's fiction, but they remain unfocused. The war is still an irrelevant part of them—irrelevant because it was too easy to blame the war for the hero's state of mind, when probably Babe Gladwaller had an incipient case of banana fever. It took Salinger some years to define Babe's feelings as a disease, to recognize, in other words, that so-called normal people were not affected with these strange symptoms of chronic hypersensitivity and sense of loss.

With the publication of his stories in the *New Yorker*, beginning with "A Perfect Day for Bananafish," he makes his first inroads into understanding. In "Bananafish," his awareness that his hero is "diseased" is still intuitive, I think. Although the "bananafish" metaphor is brilliant in itself, the insight is somewhat neutralized by Salinger's apparent blame of the wife and the mother-in-law for Seymour's suicide. The two women are, at any rate, mercilessly satirized in the telephone conversation through the mother-in-law's constant interruption of the impassioned discussion of Seymour's perilous mental health with questions like "How's your blue coat?" and "How's your ballerina?" As a result, Seymour seems as clear a victim of an external force, namely, the bourgeois matriarchy, as Babe Gladwaller was of "the war." When the important bananafish symbol

arrives later in the story, it is impossible to do much with it. There is no demonstrated connection between society's insensitivity and Seymour's zaniness.

The problem recurs again in the next story, "Uncle Wiggily in Connecticut," but not without growing evidence that Salinger is ready to resist the easy
answer that the bourgoisie and/or the war is responsible for the bananafish's
condition. Here, for example, it is quite clear that it is Eloise Wengler's tor-
menting memories of her lost lover, Walter, that make her unable to swim out of
the cave into her proper place in Exurbia. Although "the war" is a factor in her
despair since her lover is killed in it, he dies not in battle but in an "absurd"
camp accident; likewise, her militantly bourgeois husband may contribute to her
unhappiness, but she is allowed to repay him in kind. No mere victim of society,
Eloise is a bitch, not only with her husband, but with her daughter and her maid
as well. She takes the revenges of an invalid.

This story contains the first clear explanation of banana fever: it is the
sense of what is missing that causes the suffering. Here, the lover's death brings
the loss. Death, of course, is the most primitive way of making loss concrete; it is
the villain of the war stories and it is still the villain here. In "Uncle Wiggily,"
however, we have Salinger's first sign of awareness that this sense of loss ought to
be overcome, the first sign, in other words, that remembering too much is a bad
thing. Eloise, for example, resents her daughter's habit of inventing invisible
playmates, Mickey Mickeranno and Jimmy Jimmereeno, to take to bed with her
at night. Unconsciously, Eloise knows that Walter, her lost lover, is as invisible as
Ramona's boyfriends. She forces Ramona to move into the middle of the bed to
prevent her daughter from lying with an invisible lover, as she has had to lie with
one in the years since Walter's death. She knows the consequences: her bitchiness.

These "consequences" show that Salinger was not yet willing to settle
completely for a story about somebody with banana fever. In the war, he learned
that actions not only had social causes but also social consequences, so he must
indicate that Eloise's unhappiness affects others. In this way he absolved himself
from having written an isolated, clinical report about one of the hypersensitive.

                                       III

After "Uncle Wiggily," the desire to blame somebody or something generally vanishes. No longer was the evil out there somewhere; rather it was a
microbe within us. We were not oppressed; we were sick.

The stories of Salinger's middle period, from "Uncle Wiggily" to "Franny,"
are stories of the search for relief. Having evidently rejected impulsive suicide as
a cure ("A Perfect Day for Bananafish") and having seen the futility of trying to
forget ("Uncle Wiggily in Connecticut"), Salinger alternately considered the fol-

lowing remedies: sublimation in art ("The Laughing Man"), the barefaced denial of pain ("Pretty Mouth and Green My Eyes"), the love and understanding of parents ("Down at the Dinghy"), the love and understanding of children ("For Esmé" and *The Catcher in the Rye*), psychiatry (*The Catcher in the Rye*), a mystic vision ("De Daumier-Smith's Blue Period"), a mystic faith ("Teddy"), and a mystic slogan ("Franny"). It is interesting to note that each of the remedies seems to furnish at least a temporary restoration of balance for the protagonist.

In "For Esmé—with Love and Squalor" we have an interesting development in the record of the bananafish: Salinger allows himself his first *explicit* statement of what is wrong with his heroes. Actually, he allows Dostoyevski to make the statement for him; "Dear God, life is hell . . . Fathers and Teachers, I ponder, what is hell? I maintain it is the suffering of being unable to love." Although Dostoyevski's lament probably does not accurately describe Sergeant X's condition, nor that of Salinger's other heroes for that matter, most of whom love too much; still the God that the Sergeant requires is clearly a God of redemption, not of justice. What the bananafish needed was to be saved; where justice lay was no longer certain.

This can be seen even more sharply in *The Catcher in the Rye*, which appeared shortly after "Esmé," but which had taken ten years to complete. It is possible to trace how Holden's need for redemption grew in these years. The bright Holden-Phoebe relationship, for example, was undoubtedly conceived early. Not only does it follow closely the Babe-Mattie relationship of the Gladwaller stories, but the framework of the first bedroom scene between Holden and Phoebe appears in an early *Collier's* story called "I'm Crazy," in which Holden Caulfield is first introduced as a character. Later, part of the skating rink episode with Sally appeared in the *New Yorker*. In these early versions, it is hard to see Holden as much more than brash and irrepressible. *The Catcher* makes him both a kinder and a sicker person, no longer just a boy but with half his hair gray. The final chapter in the rest home, as well as the long and important scene with Mr. Antolini, must have been written late in the ten years.

In Antolini, the bananafish faces the demand for an agonizing judgment. Antolini has represented for Holden the last bastion of moral conscience; that is, Holden has called on Antolini in this crucial moment in his progress because Antolini "finally picked up that boy that jumped out of the window. . . . He didn't even give a damn if his coat got all bloody." This is a moral value to Holden. Also, Antolini shares Holden's sentiments about D.B.'s sellout to Hollywood. When Holden arrives at Antolini's, however, he finds his teacher half high and obviously married to a woman he does not love. Holden is bored with him and disappointed in him. His disappointment increases to revulsion when he awakens during the night to find Antolini "petting me or patting me on the goddam head." Terrified, he leaves at once. But the next morning, in thinking it over, he says, "I wondered if just maybe I was wrong about thinking he was making a flitty pass at me. I wondered if maybe he just liked to pat guys on the head when they're asleep. I mean how can you tell about that stuff for sure? You can't."

What Holden refuses to do, in effect, is to make an ultimate judgment on Mr. Antolini. The result is that the bananafish, having abandoned the emotional outlet of condemnation, grows more and more frustrated, a consequence of the acceptance of a purely esthetic frame of reference (i.e., "This seems ugly to me" or "This seems beautiful to me"). Note Holden's plaintive comment on Phoebe's last carousel ride: "It was just that she looked so damn *nice* going around and around in her blue coat and all." No absolute value can be assigned.

IV

The five stories published since *The Catcher in the Rye* ("De Daumier-Smith's Blue Period," "Teddy," "Franny," "Raise High the Roof Beam, Carpenters" and "Zooey") explore a solution for the bananafish, first, in terms of union with God and, finally, in terms of re-union with society.

The stories demonstrate that although the bananafish is incapacitated by the weight of his experience, he is also afflicted with a psychological conflict between the desire to participate in and the need to withdraw from society. He is a nonconformist, but a paralyzed one, unlike Arrowsmith, for example, who was moving full tilt toward a private goal, or Huckleberry Finn, who was making his precipitate escape away from society, unwilling to be captured. The Salinger hero, on the other hand, is carried along in the currents of his own psyche, neither toward nor away from anything. He drifts in a course more or less parallel to that of society, alternately tempted and repelled, half inclined to participate, and half inclined to withdraw.

In "De Daumier-Smith's Blue Period," the miracle regeneration of "For Esmé" recurs, this time in terms of a frankly mystical Experience. Salinger himself, only half ironically, uses the capital "e" to describe it, perhaps to indicate that it takes a momentary union with God in order to achieve a real insight into a man's relationship with his fellows.

The reconciliation to the idea of participation without illusion is pushed to fantastic new extremes in "Teddy," in some ways Salinger's most unexpected story. In "Teddy," reconciliation becomes Oriental resignation. The transition from the personal mysticism to the formal Eastern self-immolation which Teddy practices does not occur, however, without certain schizophrenic symptoms in both the form of the story and in its main character. It is the only one of

Salinger's stories that is utterly incredible, and yet he goes to his usual pains to document its reality.

What Teddy, this ten-year-old Buddha, has achieved in Salinger's bargain with the East is, of course, invulnerability, the persistent wish of all bananafish. The knowledge that De Daumier-Smith comes to by hard Experience, Teddy is granted early through mystic revelation. He then withdraws, as all great religious figures have, to be better able to participate. In Teddy's case, he removes himself from the boorish concerns of a society represented by his father and sister in order that he may be invulnerable to the malice of his father and sister, and be able to do good in return. He writes in his diary, for example: "See if you can find daddy's army dog tags and wear them whenever possible. It won't kill you and he will like it."

The recent publication of "Franny" revived the dilemma of participation or withdrawal. Here, the Zen Buddhist material is not as well integrated on a story level as in "Teddy," since Franny merely wishes to believe in a way of living the validity of which Teddy has had satisfactory mystic revelation. But because the tension is more psychological in "Franny," and because God is sought this side of oblivion, it is a more touching story.

In the main scene in the restaurant with her boyfriend, Franny is graphically split between the desire to withdraw and the need to participate. She has arrived to spend the weekend with Lane, already apprehensive that she will find the kind of insensitivity she has found in him many times before. She would like to be the good-time girl that Lane wants, but this time she cannot bear his egocentricity, his counterfeit participation in the world. She retreats to the stall in the ladies' room to weep for him and for all the others, one presumes, who, like Lane, are devoted to the Flaubertian view of society, that mean focus on personal vanity, which so offends Franny. Franny, a bananafish, sees all the beautiful possibilities instead, and she suffers for it. She tries to communicate with him again, finally withdraws once more and falls insensible to the ground. Her courage, however, has touched something in the boy at last. After her final collapse, he is kind to her, half understanding, but she ends making her final whispered appeal to God.

Pity for the bananafish ends with "Franny." The function of Salinger's two most recent stories, both long, didactic, and largely unsymmetrical, is to restore the stature of the bananafish. In "Raise High the Roof Beam, Carpenters," he removes the shame from the disease by showing Seymour Glass as a superior man. In "Zooey," he shows that reconciliation with society is possible if the bananafish, with courage, practices the act of Christian love.

"Raise High the Roof Beam, Carpenters" affirms the bananafish in spite of the fact that the reader knows that Seymour Glass is to end as Teddy did, embracing death. Its very title, first of all, is a paean for the bridegroom, a singularly appropriate symbol for all the Salinger heroes, who are young people, people uninitiated, unconsummated, unassimilated. The story thus is a celebration of experiences, rather than a dirge for them. Moreover, it celebrates for the first time, the sensitivity of the hero, marking perhaps a final surrender of the author's identification with the hero and a beginning of appreciation for him. If Seymour is a sick man, he is also a big man and that becomes an important thing here.

While the story explains the suicide of Seymour in "Bananafish," it also makes that suicide seem a little irrelevant. It is Seymour's life, his unique way of looking at things that concerns Salinger here, and although he is obliged to mention the subsequent death of Seymour early in the story, he refers to it simply as "death," rather than suicide. For a change, the remark seems incidental, rather than a calculated understatement, the device Salinger consistently uses when he talks about what touches him particularly.

Concerned with Seymour's life rather than his death, Salinger is at last able to expose the bananafish here. Banana fever no longer seems the shame that it did in "Pretty Mouth," "The Laughing Man," "For Esmé," and in "A Perfect Day for Bananafish" itself where Seymour can express himself only to a little girl, and ambiguously at that. The secretly prying eyes of others he is unable to bear. Witness the curious scene on the elevator when he accuses a woman in the car of staring at his feet. This happens less than a minute before he puts a bullet through his head.

In "Raise High the Roof Beam, Carpenters," the frank advocacy of Seymour enables Salinger to transcend the limits of the tight pseudopoetic structure which hamstrings so much of modern short fiction. Because the story is partisan, it must be analytic as well as metaphoric. No longer deceived into thinking his characters are prey to simple grief or to bourgeois insensitivity, rather than to beauty, he is able to expose them at last. The loosening of form, which begins with "Esmé," culminates with Seymour's throwing the stone at Charlotte, the affirmation of the effort for expression and communication even at the expense of exposure and pain.

Finally, it takes Zooey, in the story which bears his name, to communicate the new awareness and to act upon it. The redeeming union with the divine is the same as union with society, Zooey believes. If Buddy remains unreconstructable, Zooey, the youngest Glass son, comes to recognize that to be a deaf-mute in a high silk hat or a catcher in the rye is not the privilege of many.

Essentially, Zooey is a man of action. Appropriately enough, his profession is acting. Although he does not care much for a great deal of the world, he participates in it. He performs in television scripts which he detests; he meets people for lunch he does not like; he argues with his mother; he challenges his sister; he even dares to deface the shrine of the long-dead Seymour. In none of these things is he remotely self-immolating or contemplative, in the manner of Teddy; in none of them does he seek an "affinity." It is suggested that it is because Zooey alone among the Glasses has "forgiven" Seymour for his suicide that he is enabled to take a more involving and distinctly Western view of society. Zooey's final advice to his sister Franny, who has had aspirations to the stage, is: "The only thing you can do now, the only re*li*gious thing you can do, is *act*. Act for God, if you want to—be *God's* actress, if you want to. What could be prettier? You can at least try to, if you want to—there's nothing wrong in *try*ing."

Action then is the remedy here, and although remedies come and go in Salinger, it is perhaps most important because when action becomes an end in itself, it becomes possible to distinguish again between the deed and the doer. Zooey remonstrates with Franny about it: "What I don't like—and what I don't think either Seymour or Buddy would like *either*, as a matter of fact—is the way you talk about all these people. I mean you just don't despise what they represent —you despise them. It's too damn personal, Franny. I mean it." Zooey's aim is to recognize that principles exist by which men live; and that without action, things are neither good nor bad. Principles vanish. The bananafish's mind is full of still photographs; action thaws these photographs; action again makes judgments possible. It forestalls the rapt contemplation of moments that have no meaning to others and which tend to isolate each individual in his own picture gallery. To transcend the particular for the sake of the general is to overcome the paralyzed moment for the sake of the principle which animates it.

Although this is a new step for Salinger, one must observe that throughout the story, he keeps Buddy's opinion in abeyance. In the speech quoted above, Zooey suggests that Buddy and Seymour agree with him about the distinction between the deed and the doer. But the shadow of Buddy and Seymour would suggest otherwise. Zooey's consent to participate is as much rebellion from as it is practice of the way of life of his older brothers. As a matter of cold fact, principles have always gotten in the way for the bananafish because principles, ideas, systems are too far away from life as the bananafish lives it. That is why every participation in the social system has turned out to be counterfeit in the end.

V

Where Salinger fits in the mainstream of American fiction remains uncertain. As I have noted earlier, his is not what is ordinarily termed social fiction, except insofar as all novels and short stories must concern themselves with the fabric of human relations. The "disease" which I have discussed at length is innate, not social, and society's reaction to it hardly affects its virulence. If anything, society is a palliative force. Occasionally, a hero like De Daumier-Smith becomes infected with the health of society. For those who remain in the sanitarium, the remedies are many, but the truly sick seldom recover. Like Camille, they cough their way through their eternal confinement—not brave, but sometimes witty invalids, hating the disease that Salinger has diagnosed, even as Fitzgerald had diagnosed Gatsby's.

Call the disease Illusion or Delusion, Salinger stands, in regard to the nature of his insight, as close to Fitzgerald as he does to any American author. Both are concerned with the effect of the immaculate moment on men. These moments are so complete in themselves that better balanced heroes could assimilate them as the minor esthetic experiences which the "well adjusted" know them to be. Fitzgerald has always emphasized the ideational attraction. That the response of Gatsby to Daisy, of Avery to Rosalind, of Dick Diver to Nicole, and of Anthony West to Gloria is hardly sexual at all has been generally recognized. Attraction arises out of a conceptual ideal that some men have, the kind that Goethe's Werther had over a century earlier, and that Salinger's heroes were to have a generation later.

Salinger, in resisting the dominant trend of determinism in American fiction during the last fifty years, has simply succeeded a little better than Fitzgerald in isolating the hero's response by keeping the "passion" as remote from sexual connotation as possible. Where the object of delight is found in women, these women are often little girls or nuns, and what is admired is sexless in essence, some capacity for charity or candor, sensitivity or simplicity. Fitzgerald's heroes, on the other hand, usually confused glamor with beauty. To this extent, they were far more conditioned by a particular social climate than Salinger's are. If, however, they mistook Duessa for Una more often than not, it was not because they were especially at fault, but because the ideal had been corrupted by the Zeitgeist. One is compelled to feel that Fitzgerald would have been as sympathetic to Gatsby as Goethe was to Werther and as Salinger is to Seymour Glass if only Daisy Buchanan had been less obviously phony.

Fitzgerald moralizes because Daisy is a social by-product. Salinger, in his best work, does not because he sees that the terrible fascination with other human beings is apart from any good-ness or bad-ness in society as a whole or in particular individuals. This attitude places him at a little distance from Fitzgerald, and, of course, at a great distance from other American writers who have handled "fatal fascination" with traditional Puritanism, assuming that what was fascinating was necessarily either voluptuous or evil or both. Authors from Hawthorne and Poe all the way down to Faulkner are victims of this fallacy, but Salinger is not.

For this reason, Goethe's Werther (whom Salinger himself mentions in "The Girl I Knew") seems to be a more likely forbear of the bananafish than anybody in our own literature. Werther was distracted by what was fair. Plain enough. So was Tristan. And in modern German fiction, so is Thomas Mann's Aschenbach in *Death in Venice*. In each case, there is an effort to estheticize the passion, that is, to idealize its object, to see it perhaps for the purposes of the story as the hero sees it. This is Romantic, of course, and with the concomitant additions of irony, peculiarly German-Romantic—a habit of mind which many regard as archaically self-indulgent.

A part of Thomas Mann's subject matter—disease and the nonconformist, as treated in *Death in Venice*, *Tonio Kröger*, *Little Herr Friedmann*, and in much of *The Magic Mountain* and *Buddenbrooks*—is the whole of Salinger's. Both explore the nonconformist's ambivalent attitudes toward bourgeois society. Stylistically both write with wit, with a gift for the well-turned phrase and a lack of timorousness about didacticism. Allowing that Salinger has neither the intellect nor the creative energy of Mann, it seems reasonable to suppose he could benefit from the security of a form and a tradition more sympathetic to his genius than our own: for all his fidelity to the native idiom and the native scene, Salinger, like his characters, is himself hardly more than a "visitor in this garden of enamel urinals."

ALFRED KAZIN

J. D. Salinger:
"Everybody's Favorite"

The publication of his two well-known stories from the *New Yorker* in book form, *Franny and Zooey* (Little, Brown), brings home the fact that, for one reason or another, J. D. Salinger now figures in American writing as a special case. After all, there are not many writers who could bring out a book composed of two stories—both of which have already been read and argued over and analyzed to death by that enormous public of sophisticated people which radiates from the *New Yorker* to every English department in the land. Yet Salinger's fascination for this public is so great that, although he has refused this book to every book club, it may yet sell as if it were being pushed by book clubs. Since 1953, when *The Catcher in the Rye* was reprinted as a paperback, it has become the favorite American novel on the required or suggested reading lists of American colleges and secondary schools, and it has sold well over a million and a half copies. No less unusual is the fact that the *New Yorker*—which, if it did not originate, certainly brought to perfection the kind of tight, allusive, ironic story with which Salinger's earlier stories (reprinted in *Nine Stories*, 1953) felt so much at home—published in "Zooey" (41,130 words) the longest story it had ever published, and a story for which the *New Yorker* obviously felt personal affection and some particular intellectual sympathy.

In one form or another, as a fellow novelist commented unlovingly, Salinger is "everybody's favorite." He is certainly a favorite of the *New Yorker*, which in 1959 published another long story around the Glass family called "Seymour: An Introduction" (almost 30,000 words), and thus gave the impression of stretching and remaking itself to Salinger's latest stories, which have been appearing, like

From *The Atlantic Monthly* 208, no. 2 (August 1961). © 1961 by Alfred Kazin.

visits from outer space, at two-year intervals. But above all, he is a favorite with that audience of students, student intellectuals, instructors, and generally literary, sensitive, and sophisticated young people who respond to him with a consciousness that he speaks for them and virtually *to* them, in a language that is peculiarly honest and their own, with a vision of things that captures their most secret judgments of the world. The only thing that Salinger does not do for this audience is to meet with them. Holden Caulfield said in *The Catcher in the Rye* that "What really knocks me out is a book that, when you're all done reading it, you wish the author that wrote it was a terrific friend of yours and you could call him up on the phone whenever you felt like it." It is well for him that all the people in this country who now regard J. D. Salinger as a "terrific friend" do not call him up and reach him.

A fundamental reason for Salinger's appeal (like that of Hemingway in the short stories that made *him* famous) is that he has exciting professional mastery of a peculiarly charged and dramatic medium, the American short story. At a time when so much American fiction has been discursive in tone, careless in language, lacking in edge and force—when else would it have been possible for crudities like the Beat novelists to be taken seriously?—Salinger has done an honest and stimulating professional job in a medium which, when it is expertly handled, projects emotion like a cry from the stage and in form can be as intense as a lyric poem. A short story which is not handled with necessary concentration and wit is like a play which does not engage its audience; a story does not exist unless it hits its mark with terrific impact. It is a constant projection of meanings at an audience, and it is a performance minutely made up of the only possible language, as a poem is. In America, at least, where, on the whole, the best stories are the most professional stories and so are published in the most famous magazines, second-rate stories belong in the same limbo with unsuccessful musical comedies; unless you hit the bull's-eye, you don't score.

This does not mean that the best-known stories are first-rate pieces of literature any more than that so many triumphant musical comedies are additions to the world's drama; it means only that a story has communicated itself with entire vividness to its editor and its audience. The profundity that may exist in a short story by Chekhov or Tolstoy also depends upon the author's immediate success in conveying his purpose. Even in the medieval tale, which Tolstoy in his greatest stories seems to recapture in tone and spirit, the final comment on human existence follows from the deliberate artlessness of tone that the author has managed to capture like a speech in a play.

What makes Salinger's stories particularly exciting is his intense, his almost compulsive need to fill in each inch of his canvas, each moment of his scene.

Many great novels owe their grandeur to a leisurely sense of suggestion, to the imitation of life as a boundless road or flowing river, to the very relaxation of that intensity which Poe thought was the aesthetic perfection of a poem or a story. But whatever the professional superficiality of the short story in American hands, which have molded and polished it so as to reach, dazzle, and on occasion deceive the reader, a writer like Salinger, by working so hard to keep his tiny scene alive, keeps everything humming.

Someday there will be learned theses on "The Use of the Ash Tray in J. D. Salinger's Stories"; no other writer has made so much of Americans lighting up, reaching for the ash tray, setting up the ash tray with one hand while with the other they reach for a ringing telephone. Ours is a society complicated with many appliances, and Salinger always tells you what his characters are doing with each of their hands. In one long stretch of "Zooey," he describes that young man sitting in a bathtub, reading a long letter from his brother, and smoking; he manages to describe every exertion made and every sensation felt in that bathtub by the young man whose knees made "dry islands." Then the young man's mother comes into the bathroom; he draws the shower curtains around the tub, she rearranges the medicine cabinet, and while they talk (in full), everything they do is described. Everything, that is, within Salinger's purpose in getting at such detail, which is not the loose, shuffling catalogue of the old-fashioned naturalists, who had the illusion of reproducing the whole world, but the tension of a dramatist or theater director making a fuss about a character's walking just so.

For Salinger, the expert performer and director (brother Buddy Glass, who is supposed to be narrating "Zooey," speaks of "directing" it and calls the story itself a "prose home movie"), gesture is the essence of the medium. A short story does not offer room enough for the development of character; it can present only character itself, by gesture. And Salinger is remarkable, I would say he is almost frenetically proficient, in getting us, at the opening of "Franny," to *see* college boys waiting on a train platform to greet their dates arriving for a big football weekend. They rush out to the train, "most of them giving the impression of having at least three lighted cigarettes in each hand." He knows exactly how Franny Glass would be greeted by Lane Coutell: "It was a station-platform kiss—spontaneous enough to begin with, but rather inhibited in the follow-through, and with something of a forehead-bumping aspect."

And even better is his description of the boy at a good restaurant, taking a first sip of his martini and then looking "around the room with an almost palpable sense of well-being at finding himself (he must have been sure no one could dispute) in the right place with an unimpeachably right-looking girl." Salinger knows how to prepare us with this gesture for the later insensitivity of a

boy who is exactly one of those elaborately up-to-date and anxiously sophisticated people whom Franny Glass, pure in heart, must learn to tolerate, and even
to love, in what she regards as an unbearably shallow culture.

But apart from this, which is the theme of *Franny and Zooey*, the gesture
itself is recognized by the reader not only as a compliment to himself but as a
sign that Salinger is working all the time, not merely working to get the reader
to see, but working to make his scene itself hum with life and creative observation. I don't know how much this appearance of intensity on the part of Salinger,
of constant as well as full coverage, is due to *New Yorker* editorial nudging,
since its famous alertness to repetitions of words and vagueness of diction tends
to give an external look of freshness and movement to prose. Salinger not only
works very hard indeed over each story, but he obviously writes to and for some
particular editorial mind he identifies with the *New Yorker*; look up the stories
he used to write for the *Saturday Evening Post* and *Cosmopolitan*, and you will
see that just as married people get to look alike by reproducing each other's
facial expressions, so a story by Salinger and a passage of commentary in the
New Yorker now tend to resemble each other.

But whatever the enormous influence of any magazine on those who write
regularly for it, Salinger's emphasis of certain words and syllables in American
speech and his own compulsiveness in bearing down hard on certain details
(almost as if he wanted to make the furniture, like the gestures of certain people,
tell *everything* about the people who use them) do give his stories the intensity
of observation that is fundamental to his success. Lane Coutell, sitting in that
restaurant with Franny and talking about a college paper on Flaubert he is
horribly well satisfied with, says,

> I think the emphasis I put on *why* he was so neurotically attached to
> the *mot juste* wasn't too bad. I mean in the light of what we know
> today. Not just psychoanalysis and all that crap, but certainly to a
> certain extent. You know what I mean. I'm no Freudian man or
> anything like that, but certain things you can't just pass over as
> capital-F Freudian and let them go at that. I mean to a certain extent
> I think I was perfectly justified to point out that none of the really
> good boys—Tolstoy, Dostoevski, *Shake*speare, for Chrissake—were
> such goddam word-squeezers. They just wrote. Know what I mean?

What strikes me about this mimicry is not merely that it is so clever, but that it is
also so relentless. In everything that this sophisticated ass, Lane Coutell, says,
one recognizes that he is and will be wrong. Salinger disapproves of him in the
deepest possible way; he is a spiritual enemy.

Of course, it is a vision of things that lies behind Salinger's expert manner.

There is always one behind every manner. The language of fiction, whatever it may accomplish as representation, ultimately conveys an author's intimation of things; makes us hear, not in a statement, but in the ensemble of his realized efforts, his quintessential commentary on the nature of existence. However, the more deliberate the language of the writer, as it must be in a short story, the more the writer must convey his judgment of things in one highlighted dramatic action, as is done on the stage.

At the end of "Franny," the young girl collapses in the ladies' room of the restaurant where she has been lunching with her cool boyfriend. This conveys her spiritual desperation in his company, for Lane typifies a society where "Everything everybody does is so—I don't know—not *wrong*, or even mean, or even stupid necessarily. But just so tiny and meaningless and—sad-making." Her brother Zooey (Zachary Glass), at the end of the long second story, calls her up from another telephone number in the same apartment and somehow reaches to the heart of her problem and gives her peace by reminding her that the "Fat Lady" they used to picture somnolently listening to them when they were quiz kids on the radio—the ugly, lazy, even disgusting-looking Fat Lady, who more and more typifies unattractive and selfish humanity in our day—can be loved after all, for she, too, is Jesus Christ.

In each story, the climax bears a burden of meaning that it would not have to bear in a novel; besides being stagy, the stories are related in a way that connects both of them into a single chronicle. This, to quote the title of a little religious pamphlet often mentioned in it, might be called "The Way of a Pilgrim." Both Franny and Zooey Glass are, indeed, pilgrims seeking their way in a society typified by the Fat Lady, and even by Lane Coutell's meaningless patter of sophistication. No wonder Franny cries out to her unhearing escort: "I'm sick of just liking people. I wish to God I could meet somebody I could respect." The Glasses (mother Irish, father Jewish) are ex-vaudevillians whose children were all, as infant prodigies, performers on a radio quiz program called "It's a Wise Child." Now, though engaged in normally sophisticated enterprises (Franny goes to a fashionable women's college, Zooey is a television actor, Buddy a college instructor), they have retained their intellectual precocity—and, indeed, their precocious charm—and have translated, as it were, their awareness of themselves as special beings into a conviction that they alone can do justice to their search for the true way.

The eldest and most brilliant of the children, Seymour, shot himself in 1948 while on his honeymoon in Florida; this was the climax of Salinger's perhaps most famous story, "A Perfect Day for Bananafish." And it is from Seymour's old room in the Glass apartment that Zooey calls up his sister, Franny, on a phone that is normally never used, that is still listed in the name of Seymour

Glass, and that has been kept up by Buddy (who does not want a phone in his own country retreat) and by Zooey in order to perpetuate Seymour's name and to symbolize his continuing influence on them as a teacher and guide. It is from reading over again, in Seymour's old room, various religious sayings from the world's literature that Seymour had copied out on a piece of beaverboard nailed to the back of a door that Zooey is inspired to make the phone call to Franny that ends with the revelation that the horrible Fat Lady is really Jesus Christ.

This final episode, both in the cuteness of its invention and in the cuteness of speech so often attributed to Seymour, who is regarded in his own family as a kind of guru, or sage, helps us to understand Salinger's wide popularity. I am sorry to have to use the word "cute" in respect to Salinger, but there is absolutely no other word that for me so accurately typifies the self-conscious charm and prankishness of his own writing and his extraordinary cherishing of his favorite Glass characters.

Holden Caulfield is also cute in *The Catcher in the Rye*, cute in his little-boy suffering for his dead brother, Allie, and cute in his tenderness for his sister, "Old Phoebe." But we expect that boys of that age may be cute—that is, consciously appealing and consciously clever. To be these things is almost their only resource in a world where parents and schoolmasters have all the power and the experience. Cuteness, for an adolescent, is to turn the normal self-pity of children, which arises from their relative weakness, into a relative advantage vis-à-vis the adult world. It becomes a role boys can play in the absence of other advantages, and *The Catcher in the Rye* is so full of Holden's cute speech and cute innocence and cute lovingness for his own family that one must be an absolute monster not to like it.

And on a higher level, but with the same conscious winsomeness, the same conscious mournfulness and intellectual loneliness and lovingness (though not for his wife), Seymour Glass is cute when he sits on the beach with a little girl telling her a parable of "bananafish"—ordinary-looking fish when "they swim into a hole where there's a lot of bananas," but "after that they're so fat they can't get out of the hole again. . . . They die." His wife, meanwhile busy in their room on the long-distance phone to her mother in New York, makes it abundantly clear in the hilariously accurate cadences and substance of her conversation why her husband finds it more natural to talk to a four-year-old girl on the beach than to her. Among other things, Seymour expects not to be understood outside the Glass family. But agonizing as this situation is, the brilliantly entertaining texture of "A Perfect Day for Bananafish" depends on Seymour Glass's conscious cleverness as well as on his conscious suffering—even his conscious cleverness *about* the suffering of "ordinary-looking" fish who get so bloated eating too many bananas in a "hole" they shouldn't have been attracted to in the first place.

In the same way, not only does the entertaining surface of *Franny and Zooey* depend on the conscious appealingness and youthfulness and generosity and sensitivity of Seymour's brother and sister, but Salinger himself, in describing these two, so obviously feels such boundless affection for them that you finally get the sense of all these child prodigies and child entertainers being tied round and round with veils of self-love in a culture which they—and Salinger—just despise. Despise, above all, for its intellectual pretentiousness. Yet this is the society, typified by the Fat Lady (symbolically, they pictured her as their audience), whom they must now force themselves to think of as Jesus Christ, and whom, as Christ Himself, they can now at last learn to love.

For myself, I must confess that the spiritual transformation that so many people associate with the very sight of the word "love" on the printed page does not move me as it should. In what has been considered Salinger's best story, "For Esmé—with Love and Squalor," Sergeant X in the American Army of Occupation in Germany is saved from a hopeless breakdown by the beautiful magnanimity and remembrance of an aristocratic young English girl. We are prepared for this climax or visitation by an earlier scene in which the sergeant comes upon a book by Goebbels in which a Nazi woman had written, "Dear God, life is hell." Under this, persuaded at last of his common suffering even with a Nazi, X writes down, from *The Brothers Karamazov*: "Fathers and teachers, I ponder 'What is hell?' I maintain that it is the suffering of being unable to love."

But the love that Father Zossima in Dostoyevski's novel speaks for is surely love for the world, for God's creation itself, for all that precedes us and supports us, that will outlast us and that alone helps us to explain ourselves to ourselves. It is the love that D. H. Lawrence, another religious novelist, spoke of as "the sympathetic bond" and that in one form or another lies behind all the great novels as a primary interest in everyone and everything alive with us on this common earth. The love that Salinger's horribly precocious Glass characters speak of is love for certain people only—forgiveness is for the rest; finally, through Seymour Glass's indoctrination of his brothers and sister in so many different (and pretentiously assembled) religious teachings, it is love of certain ideas. So what is ultimate in their love is the love of their own moral and intellectual excellence, of their chastity and purity in a world full of bananafish swollen with too much food. It is the love that they have for themselves as an idea.

The worst they can say about our society is that they are too sensitive to live in it. They are the special case in whose name society is condemned. And what makes them so is that they are young, precocious, sensitive, different. In

Salinger's work, the two estates—the world and the cutely sensitive young—never really touch at all. Holden Caulfield condemns parents and schools because he knows that they are incapable of understanding him; Zooey and Franny and Buddy (like Seymour before them) know that the great mass of prosperous spiritual savages in our society will never understand them.

This may be true, but to think so can lead to a violation of art. Huckleberry Finn, so often cited as a parallel to the hero of *The Catcher in the Rye*, was two years younger than Holden, but the reason he was not afraid of an adult's world is that he had respect for it. He had never even seen very much of it until he got on that raft with a runaway Negro slave he came to love and was able to save. It was still all God's creation, and inspired him with wonder. But Holden and, even more, the Glass children are beaten before they start; beaten in order not to start. They do not trust anything or anyone but themselves and their great idea. And what troubles me about this is not what it reflects of their theology but what it does to Salinger's art.

Frank O'Connor once said of this special métier, the short story, that it is "the art form that deals with the individual when there is no longer a society to absorb him, and when he is compelled to exist, as it were, by his own inner light." This is the condition on which Salinger's work rests, and I should be sorry to seem unsympathetic toward it. It is an American fact, as one can see from the relative lack in our literature of the ripe and fully developed social novel in which the individual and society are in concrete and constant relationship with each other. But whatever this lack, which in one sense is as marked in the novels of Scott Fitzgerald as it is in Salinger's emphasis upon the short story, it is a fact that when Fitzgerald describes a character's voice, it is because he really loves—in the creative sense, is fully interested in—this character. When Salinger describes a character's voice, it is to tell us that the man is a phony. He has, to borrow a phrase from his own work, a "categorical aversion" to whole classes and types of our society. The "sympathetic bond" that Lawrence spoke of has been broken. People stink in our nostrils. We are mad with captious observation of one another. As a friend of mine once said about the novels of Mary McCarthy, trying to say with absolute justice what it was that shocked her so much in them, "The heroine is always right and everyone else is wrong." Salinger is a far more accomplished and objective writer of fiction than Mary McCarthy, but I would say that in his work the Glass children alone are right and everyone else is wrong.

And it is finally this condition, not just the famous alienation of Americans from a society like our own, that explains the popularity of Salinger's work. Salinger's vast public, I am convinced, is based not merely on the vast number of young people who recognize their emotional problems in his fiction and their frustrated rebellions in the sophisticated language he manipulates so skillfully. It is based perhaps even more on the vast numbers who have been released by our society to think of themselves as endlessly sensitive, spiritually alone, gifted, and whose suffering lies in the narrowing of their consciousness to themselves, in the withdrawal of their curiosity from a society which they think they understand all too well, in the drying up of their hope, their trust, and their wonder at the great world itself. The worst of American sophistication today is that it is so bored, so full of categorical aversion to things that writers should never take for granted and never close their eyes to.

The fact that Salinger's work is particularly directed against the "well fed sun-burned" people at the summer theater, at the "section men" in colleges parroting the latest fashionable literary formulas, at the "three-martini" men— this, indeed, is what is wrong. He hates them. They are no longer people, but symbols, like the Fat Lady. No wonder that Zooey tells his sister: Love them, love them all, love them anyway! But the problem is not one of spiritual pride or of guilt; it is that in the tearing of the "sympathetic bond" it is not love that goes, but the deepest possibilities of literary art.

DAVID D. GALLOWAY

The Love Ethic

Few heroes of contemporary literature have aroused so much devotion, imitation, or controversy as J. D. Salinger's Holden Caulfield, the disaffiliated adolescent whose lost weekend in New York is chronicled in *The Catcher in the Rye*. As an impressionable adolescent making his first tentative movements into an adult world, Holden becomes a sensitive register by which the values of that world can be judged. From the opening pages of this novel the world is seen to be fragmentary, distorted, and absurd—in Holden's own special vernacular, "phony." It is an environment in which real communication on a sensitive level is impossible, and when Holden unsuccessfully tries to explain his spiritual pain to Sally Hayes, there is certainly more than a coincidental suggestion of Eliot's "J. Alfred Prufrock" in the frustrated cry, " 'You don't see what I meant at all.' "

Holden does not refuse to grow up so much as he agonizes over the state of being grown up. The innocent world of childhood is amply represented in *The Catcher in the Rye*, but Holden, as a frustrated, disillusioned, anxious hero, stands for modern man rather than merely for the modern adolescent. He is self-conscious and often ridiculous, but he is also an anguished human being of special sensitivity. Even though he is often childishly ingenuous, and his language is frequently comic, Holden must be seen as both a representative and a critic of the modern environment, as the highly subjective tone of the novel suggests.

As a misfit Holden has literary predecessors in such early Salinger stories as "The Hang of It," "The Varioni Brothers," "Soft-Boiled Sergeant," "This Sandwich Has No Mayonnaise," and "The Stranger." Holden is not unlike Rabbit Angstrom or Augie March in seeking the environment in which he can perform

From *The Absurd Hero in American Fiction*. © 1966 by David D. Galloway. University of Texas Press, 1966.

at his best, and the result is a painful contemporary odyssey. As the novel opens, Holden is in the process of rejecting yet another uncongenial environment, Pencey Prep. There he feels surrounded by phonies, just as he had felt surrounded by them at Elkton Hills, his previous school: "One of the biggest reasons I left Elkton Hills was because I was surrounded by phonies. That's all. They were coming in the goddam window." That "Goddam Elkton Hills" is far more than an example of the social snobbery of an Eastern prep school. It comes to stand for a world in which values and perspectives have become so distorted that there seems little if any room for the sensitive individual who attempts to order the flux of human existence or to bring it into the light of a consistent aesthetic perspective. To this significant degree, the milieu in which Salinger heroes function is "absurd." Like Camus's absurd man, the Salinger hero tries to live by ethical standards in an indifferent, often nihilistic universe. An important distinction, however, must be drawn between Camus's absurd man and the absurd man in Salinger's fiction. This distinction is primarily one of consciousness, for Camus's heroes consciously acknowledge the absurdity of their struggle against reality. While the reader is in a position to see the absurdity of Holden's quixotic gestures and of Zooey's ultimate, transcendent "love" stance, he is never entirely certain that the characters themselves see their own struggles as absurd, though Zooey at least approaches this essential awareness. These characters, however, do demonstrate "disproportions" on the level of values which make the myth of the absurd applicable to their struggles. The context of the absurd does not perhaps explain as much about Salinger as it did about Updike, Styron, or Bellow, but it does help us to see what Salinger has tried to accomplish in his writing and to understand his relationship to other contemporary novelists.

Few areas of modern life escape Holden Caulfield's indictment. Among those most severely challenged are the movies (to which his brother D.B., a writer, has prostituted himself) and religious enthusiasm. Holden explains that the children in his family are all "atheists" because his parents are of different religious persuasions (foreshadowing the Irish-Jewish Glass family). Thus Holden's biting but revealing point of view is not clouded by specific religious commitments, and he can love the nuns whom he meets in Grand Central Station even though he feels that Catholicism usually throws up insurmountable barriers to communication. Just as he loves the nuns for their simplicity and honesty, he sees through the selfish religious pose of "this guy Ossenburger," an undertaker who contributes a dormitory wing to Pencey.

The phoniness of Hollywood and of religion as it is often practiced in the contemporary world come together to form a dramatic whole in the Christmas pageant which Holden attends at Radio City. Following the Rockettes and a man who roller-skated under tables, "they had this Christmas thing they have at Radio City every year":

> All these angels start coming out of the boxes and everywhere, guys
> carrying crucifixes and stuff all over the place, and the whole bunch
> of them—*thousands* of them—singing "Come All Ye Faithful!"
> like mad. Big deal. It's supposed to be religious as hell, I know, and
> very pretty and all, but I can't see anything religious or pretty, for
> God's sake, about a bunch of actors carrying crucifixes all over the
> stage.

The blatant, graceless *kitsch* of the movie which follows the stage show (and which has been identified as James Hilton's *Random Harvest*) is an equally commercial deception, an artificial substitute for the love and generosity which Americans have forgotten how to express. After his experience with a Radio City Christmas, Holden feels yet more agonizingly frustrated and alone. "I'm sort of glad they've got the atomic bomb invented," he comments. "If there's ever another war, I'm going to sit right the hell on top of it. I'll volunteer for it, I swear to God I will."

Wherever Holden turns, his craving for truth seems to be frustrated by the phoniness of the world. From his hotel window he looks out upon scenes of perversion and distortion; in bars and nightclubs he hears only the laconic accents of shallow supersophisticates or self-satisfied intellectuals. When he finds innocence or purity it is always jeopardized by evil or apathy, and he searches desperately for something to sustain him. An answer seems to come from Mr. Antolini, a former English teacher who explains to Holden that the fall he is riding for is " 'a special kind of fall, a horrible kind. The man falling isn't permitted to feel or hear himself hit bottom. He just keeps falling and falling. The whole arrangement's designed for men who, at some time or other in their lives, were looking for something their own environment couldn't supply them with. So they gave up looking.' " Mr. Antolini urges Holden to continue to search in humility for a cause worth living for. Such a search, he assures Holden, has been chronicled by educated and scholarly men, and he promises to guide the boy into an intellectual channel that will both stimulate and comfort him. Whatever consolation there may have been in this message is destroyed when Holden awakens to find Mr. Antolini petting him—and he flees from yet another example of the world's perversion.

What prompts Holden's quest is his desire for unity, a desire that is expressed in the comfort and safety which he always felt in the Museum of Natural History:

> The best thing, though, in that museum was that everything always
> stayed right where it was. Nobody'd move. You could go there a
> hundred thousand times, and that Eskimo would still be just finished

catching those two fish, the birds would still be on their way south,
the deers would still be drinking out of that water hole, with their
pretty antlers and their pretty, skinny legs, and that squaw with the
naked bosom would still be weaving that same blanket. Nobody'd
be different.

That such a reassuringly ordered universe is an impossible dream is emphasized
by the fact that, when Holden visits the museum near the conclusion of his New
York odyssey, he sees the words " 'Fuck you' . . . written with a red crayon or
something, right under the glass part of the wall, under the stones." Holden
wishes to erase the interminable "Fuck you's" on all the alley walls and school
corridors and sidewalks in the world, and this intention to cancel out vulgarity
and phoniness is a poignant if naive example of the absurd.

   The Catcher in the Rye is an important articulation of one of the possible
responses which man may make to an essentially destructive life experience.
Since, Holden reasons, there is no fulfillment in the adult world, since all it can
offer man is frustration or corruption, the only worthwhile task to which he can
devote himself is that of the protector who stops children before they enter
the world of destruction and phoniness and keeps them in a state of arrested
innocence:

> "Anyway, I keep picturing all these little kids playing some game
> in this big field of rye and all. Thousands of little kids, and nobody's
> around—nobody big, I mean, except me. And I'm standing on the
> edge of some crazy cliff. What I have to do, I have to catch everybody
> if they start to go over the cliff—I mean if they're running and they
> don't look where they're going I have to come out from somewhere
> and *catch* them. That's all I'd do all day. I'd just be the catcher in
> the rye and all. I know it's crazy, but that's the only thing I'd really
> like to be. I know it's crazy."

Holden's reiteration of the word "crazy" reminds us that his ambition is also
"absurd," for his Christ-like intention (suffering the little children to come unto
him) is opposed to the reality in which children like his own sister, Phoebe, are
carted off to the Lister Foundation to see movies on euthanasia and move along
grimy school corridors which flaunt the words "Fuck you!" at them. While
Holden has a vision of his role in the world, he is unable either to live the
absurdity he has outlined or to develop an absurd faith. The reasons for this
failure on his part are simple and obvious. First, even though we are clearly
intended to see him as a representative of modern man, Holden is an adolescent,
and both his experience and his perspectives are too limited for him to offer any

kind of finalized "answer" to the phoniness of the world. Second, and perhaps most important, his vision carries within itself a destructive contradiction. While Holden's intention is absurd in its opposition to reality, the goal of his intention is to help innocent children to *avoid* reality. His conclusion negates his premise insofar as it eliminates one of the two crucial terms of the absurd confrontation and offers no formula by which man can live in and with his world. Holden's intention is moving and vaguely saintly, but it involves a nostalgia which, according to Camus, the absurd man must reject. (Indeed, Holden himself rejects it when he decides that he must not attempt to protect Phoebe during her final ride on the carousel.)

What Salinger leaves us with in this novel is an often biting image of the absurd contemporary milieu. The idea of perpetuating the innocence of child-hood is a philosophically untenable position, and the only other unrejected pro-posals in the novel are so vague that their full importance can be seen only in Salinger's later work. The first of these proposals for a stance at once self-protective and humanistically fulfilling is made by Carl Luce, who suggests a vague mystical discipline derived from Eastern philosophy as a solution to Hol-den's spiritual agony, but Luce's approach to this discipline seems supersophisti-cated and "phony." In the epilogue to the novel Holden suggests the possibility of reentering society when he says, "I sort of *miss* everybody I told about. Even old Stradlater and Ackley, for instance. I think I even miss that goddam Maurice." Holden misses even the phonies of the world because his experience has taught him something about the necessity of loving, and here Salinger sounds what is to become his major and most complex theme.

After *The Catcher in the Rye* Salinger wrote several stories examining the mystical process, and even though his mystically inclined heroes are engaging and at times inspiring, their stance must be rejected, too, in favor of a position that leads man to the world rather than to an intense but isolating subjective experience. Like efforts to recapture the innocence of childhood, mysticism (which Salinger usually considers in terms of Zen Buddhism) is finally seen as an evasion and contradiction of Western man's spiritual quest. In Zen Buddhism, the life of the mystic is only temporarily one of isolation, for after the achieve-ment of *satori*, the state of total enlightenment and consciousness that is the goal of Zen Buddhism, the enlightened man reenters the world to perform good works. Thus, Salinger's rejection of the transitory, unearned mystical *experience* is understandable in terms of its failure to provide a program which the indi-vidual can follow in order to give his life meaning, but his rejection of mysticism itself is more difficult to understand—especially in light of his own involvement with Zen Buddhism. Mysticism is treated as a "fever" in Salinger's writings, an isolating and therefore unfruitful discipline that inevitably leads Western man away from the paths of significant human involvement. Furthermore, while satori may eventually guide the Buddhist back into his world, the good works which he is prepared to perform are not necessarily those works which a spiritually enlightened Westerner should be prepared to perform. It is not through mysticism but through love that the Salinger hero at last reenters the world.

From 1945 until 1951, J. D. Salinger published sixteen short stories, several of the same slick, predictable character as the stories he wrote for popular magazines during World War II. Five of those stories, however, were concerned with Holden Caulfield and his family, and three of them represented the beginning of his largest and most serious body of work—the "saga" of the Glass family. The first of these stories centers on an elusive character named Seymour Glass, whose suicide is the subject of the first story in Salinger's second book, *Nine Stories*. Little in this brief account indicates the scope of the Glass series, but it sets the stage for the rejection of mysticism as a solution to the contemporary spiritual dilemma. In order to appreciate the strength of Salinger's rejection, one must understand his fascination with the mystical process itself. Two of Salinger's *Nine Stories*, "De Daumier-Smith's Blue Period" and "Teddy," chronicle, respectively, the mystical vision and the mystical faith.

De Daumier-Smith is the fanciful pseudonym adopted by a somewhat typical Salinger *isolatoe* who brashly attempts to create a new image of himself with which he can confront a world from which he suddenly feels disaffiliated. De Daumier-Smith's rebellion resembles Holden's in that he too is hypersensitive to the phoniness of the world, but the origin of his disaffiliation is more specifically identified as the absence of love. Jean narrates his own story, and the most pertinent fact about his childhood is that he had never truly loved anyone but his mother. Shortly after her death, he moves to New York with his stepfather. Having drawn some slight attention as an artist when his family lived in Paris, Jean embroiders his experiences, draws up an imaginary list of professional credentials and friends (including Picasso), and applies for a job as an instructor at "Les Amis Des Vieux Maîtres," a correspondence art school in Montreal. What prompts him to make this sudden "quixotic gesture" is the realization that he and his father "were both in love with the same deceased woman." This knowledge forces him out of the innocent private world in which he had formerly lived, and the very telling of his story is an attempt to give order to the experiences which greet him in the public world—a world which at first seems no more complete or fulfilling than the Oedipally narrow world in which he had previously functioned. The isolation which De Daumier-Smith suffers is underscored by the fact that we never learn his real name; he adopts a bogus identity and a preposterously contrived set of credentials in order to teach students whom he will never see in a French art school run by two Japanese. When Jean reveals to the Yoshotos that he is a student of Buddhism, they inform him that they are Presbyterians. However ambitiously ingratiating he becomes to his employers, his loneliness only increases.

What seems to offer Jean consolation is his discovery of naive beauty in the crude but talented paintings of Sister Irma of the Order of St. Joseph. In Jean's wild daydreams about the nun, she comes to represent his last chance to communicate with another sensitive spirit, and he yearns for a moment of truth and love with her which will make him spiritually whole and effect his conversion into a great healer.

When her Superior severs Sister Irma's relationship with the art school after reading Jean's passionate letter to her, the boy is cast into a painful and almost total despair; but from that dark night of the soul he passes into a period of illumination. Like the precocious members of the Glass family, Jean has been a student of comparative religions, and his study has at least partially prepared him for the epiphany which greets him and flashes like the sun into his dark night. Les Amis Des Vieux Maîtres is located over an orthopedic appliances shop, and as Jean pauses before the window, he seems to see it as a *collage* representing all of the crippling inhumanity of the world: "The thought was forced on me that no matter how coolly or sensibly or gracefully I might one day learn to live my life, I would always at best be a visitor in a garden of enamel urinals and bedpans, with a sightless, wooden dummy-deity standing by in a marked-down rupture truss." Later, however, he has what he calls an "Experience," in which everything in the window is transformed:

> Suddenly (and I say this, I believe, with all due self-consciousness), the sun came up and sped toward the bridge of my nose at the rate of ninety-three million miles a second. Blinded and very frightened—I had to put my hand on the glass to keep my balance. The thing lasted for no more than a few seconds. When I got my sight back, the girl had gone from the window, leaving behind her a shimmering field of exquisite, twice-blessed flowers.

"De Daumier-Smith's Blue Period" offers a strong suggestion that a mystical experience may help man to alter his vision of the world so significantly that he will be able to live in it. Jean de Daumier-Smith does return to the world after his dark night of despair to spend a "normal" summer of girl-watching on the beach. While Jean has something closely related to a mystical revelation, he is not a mystic: "I'd like, if possible, to avoid seeming to pass it off as a case, or even a borderline case, of genuine mysticism." While his experience offers the promise of a degree of spiritual fulfillment he had not known before, his story suggests no code by which the individual can oppose a world made up of "enamel urinals and bedpans" and ruled over by a "wooden dummy-deity." His discovery of an order and transcendent meaning in a sterile and hostile world is rather a product of chance, than the climax of experience. This situation is typical for the modern hero, to whom revelation or epiphany comes as a sudden intuitive flash, suggesting in part that visions of order or meaning are not available through reason.

In "Teddy" Salinger concerned himself with the realized mystic Teddy McArdle, a precocious ten-year-old who has achieved the enlightened consciousness of satori. Teddy's mysticism frees him from the grossness of his parents, but Salinger treats his mystic lyrically and impressionistically, never attempting to describe the process by which Teddy arrives at satori, other than by referring to the boy's intense periods of meditation, but in "A Perfect Day for Bananafish" he allegorically demonstrates that mysticism is not a solution to man's dilemma.

As we learn from later stories about the Glass family, Seymour Glass has travelled to Florida with his wife in order to "recover" from a state of acute depression. In the first half of "A Perfect Day for Bananafish," through a telephone conversation between his wife and her mother, we are given some insight into the causes of his depression. Muriel comes from a world whose main concerns are with "normalcy" and whose emotional outlets are found in the kind of melodramatic movie which to Holden Caulfield seemed a puerile commercial sham. The hotel room in which Seymour commits suicide is characterized by the smell "of new calfskin luggage and nail-lacquer remover." Without the bananafish allegory the reader might see Seymour's suicide as merely a rejection of this world of crass superficiality, but it is also—and more significantly—a rejection of the mystical life itself.

While Muriel is talking to her mother and trying to reassure her that Seymour has had no more destructive urges, Seymour is on the beach with Sybil Carpenter. He catches the young girl's attention with a variety of fantasies, the most complex of which involves the bananafish. Pushing Sybil out into the water on a rubber float, he explains to her the inherent fatalism of bananafish:

> "Well, they swim into a hole where there's a lot of bananas. They're very ordinary-looking fish when they swim *in*. But once they get in, they behave like pigs. Why, I've known some bananafish to swim into a banana hole and eat as many as seventy-eight bananas." He edged the float and its passenger a foot closer to the horizon. "Naturally, after that they're so fat they can't get out of the hole again. Can't fit through the door."

Seymour's life has been filled with erratic spiritual experiences, and to his brothers and sisters he stands as a kind of Christ-figure. Like the bananafish, however, he has become so glutted with this experience that he can no longer participate in the real world outside himself. This inability, which accounts for what he calls the "very tragic life" which the bananafish leads, is emphasized by the fact that he cannot bear the eyes of the world. After leaving Sybil on the beach, Seymour walks into the hotel elevator along with a young woman:

> "I see you're looking at my feet," he said to her when the car was
> in motion.
> "I beg your pardon?" said the woman.
> "I said I see you're looking at my feet."
> "I *beg* your pardon. I happened to be looking at the floor," said
> the woman, and faced the doors of the car.
> "If you want to look at my feet, say so," said the young man.
> "But don't be a God-damned sneak about it."

Following this episode, Seymour enters his hotel room, takes a pistol from his suitcase, and fires a bullet through his head.

Salinger rejects the mystic's experience as a solution to man's alienation in an absurd universe because mysticism ("banana fever") removes man from reality. While Seymour is never a fully realized mystic like Teddy, it is inconsistent to explain away his suicide as despair over the idea of achieving satori. Seymour has already rejected satori because it leads him out of the world in which he feels he must live, and his rejection is overt and conscious. His life has been filled with one transcendent experience after another, with visions and intense spiritual moments which affirm his ability to achieve satori. Among the reminders of such experiences, Seymour notes, "I have scars on my hands from touching certain people."

> "Once, in the park, when Franny was still in the carriage, I put
> my hand on the downy pate of her head and left it there too long.
> Another time, at Lowe's Seventy-second Street, with Zooey during a
> spooky movie. He was about six or seven, and he went under the
> seat to avoid watching a scary scene. I put my hand on his head.
> Certain heads, certain colors and textures of human hair leave per-
> manent marks on me. Other things, too. Charlotte once ran away
> from me, outside the studio, and I grabbed her dress to stop her, to
> keep her near me. A yellow cotton dress I loved because it was too
> long for her. I still have a lemon-yellow mark on the palm of my
> right hand. Oh, God, if I'm anything by a clinical name, I'm a kind
> of paranoiac in reverse. I suspect people of plotting to make me
> happy."

As we learn in "Raise High the Roof Beam, Carpenters," Seymour was so happy over his marriage to Muriel that he was unable to attend his own wedding.

Seymour's wedding-day happiness came from the thought that he might at last emerge from the spiritual "hole" into which he had begun swimming as a child. Unable to resign a quest for a miraculous spiritual perfection, and simultaneously unequipped to join the world of mere possibility, Seymour chose suicide. As Dan Wakefield has noted, suicide and miracle are the extremes between which many of Salinger's characters fluctuate, but the author's primary concern is with the alternatives which exist between those extremes. No appeal to a spiritual absolute (and no transcendent spiritual experience) is a wholly successful alternative. In his later stories Salinger turns his attention to other stances which man can make in an absurd world to give his life meaning.

   Salinger would certainly agree with Dan Wakefield's observation that ours is a time in which men are " 'no longer feeling within themselves the idol but still feeling the altar,' and the questions of what replaces the idol which once provided a set of answers for human conduct; the question of how men act with morality and love if there is no idol which prescribes the rules, is a central and vital question." Salinger begins to define his answer in "For Esmé—with Love and Squalor." The narrator of this story—who is never more fully identified than as "Sergeant X"—writes his story as a kind of epithalamium after receiving an invitation to Esmé's wedding. He had met the girl while stationed in England for special D-Day training, and the loneliness which he experienced before their meeting is idiomatic to the Salinger hero.

   On a free Saturday afternoon at the end of his training course Sergeant X walks into Devon and almost by accident enters a church in which a children's choir is rehearsing. There he becomes enchanted by Esmé, a young girl of "about thirteen, with straight, ash-blond hair of ear-lobe length, an exquisite forehead, and blasé eyes that, I thought, might very possibly have counted the house." Later Sergeant X meets the girl in a tearoom, and Esmé tries to comfort and entertain the lonely G.I. When she leaves the tearoom, it is with the request that X someday write her a story "about love and squalor."

   X's experience with squalor comes in Bavaria, where he is trying unsuccessfully to recover from his encounter with undefined battlefield horrors. His recovery is not aided by the loutish insensitivity of his companion, Clay, or by his own brother's request for wartime souvenirs: " 'How about sending the kids a couple of bayonets or swastikas . . .?' " X is quartered in a house recently confiscated from a family whose daughter was an official in the Nazi party; among the books which she has left behind is Goebbels's "Die Zeit Ohne Beispiel," a title ironically descriptive of X's condition. He opens the book to find the words " 'Dear God, life is hell' " written on the flyleaf. With a sudden energy X writes under this a passage from Dostoyevski, " 'Fathers and teachers,' I ponder, 'What is hell?' I maintain that it is the suffering of being unable to love.' " It is in this inscription that the inability to love is specifically articulated as the curse that visits Salinger's pilgrims. Later X is saved by a small package lying among the clutter of his desk, for the package represents a gesture of love which directly opposes the squalor of his world. In the package is an "extremely water-proof and shock-proof" watch which had belonged to Esmé's dead father, and which she now sends X as a lucky talisman. X sits for a long while with the watch in his hand, and "Then, suddenly, almost ecstatically, he felt sleepy. You take a really sleepy man, Esmé, and he *al*ways stands a chance of again becoming a man with all his fac—with all his f-a-c-u-l-t-i-e-s intact." The story which X writes for Esmé is itself a gesture of love (similarly, Salinger wrote one of his most important stories, "Franny," as a wedding present for his wife). The love which saves Sergeant X comes from an innocent child, but the idea of love as man's salvation, unlike the suggestion of mysticism, is not rejected, and it finally becomes developed into an absurd gesture which Salinger offers as the answer to an idol-less altar.

The absurd love gesture is chronicled in the two interrelated stories, "Franny" and "Zooey," which were originally published in the *New Yorker* and later combined and published as a book. Franny and Zooey are the youngest brother and sister of Seymour Glass, and part of the urban menagerie of sensitiveness and titanesque idiosyncrasy around which Salinger is constructing his contemporary saga. To understand how Franny and Zooey offer a resolution which Seymour and other mystically inclined heroes could not accomplish, it is necessary to know something of the relationships of this sprawling family.

There are seven Glass children—in order of birth, Seymour, Buddy, Boo Boo, the twins Walt and Waker, Zachary (Zooey), and Franny. Les and Bessie Glass, the parents, were once a famous vaudeville team (billed as "Gallagher and Glass") on the old Pantages and Orpheum circuits. Les is Jewish and Bessie Irish, and they are descended "from an astonishingly long and motley double file of professional entertainers." The public life of their parents has helped to give the Glass children an especially acute sense of the public world, and this sense is accented by the fact that all seven children began life as child prodigies on a radio quiz program called "It's a Wise Child." (Salinger is almost certainly aware of Telemachus's consciously cryptic reply to Athena when she questions him about Odysseus: "It's a wise child that knows its own father." This oblique reference to *The Odyssey* emphasizes the quest for identity on which each of the Glass children has at some point embarked.)

The story of Seymour Glass (1917–48) is told directly through "A Perfect Day for Bananafish" and indirectly through "Raise High the Roof Beam, Carpenters," "Seymour: An Introduction," and "Zooey." Buddy Glass is a shy, sardonic creative-writing teacher who occasionally takes upon himself the task of narrating his family's spiritual history. In "Seymour: An Introduction" he emerges as a *persona* for Salinger himself. In spiritual training Buddy was closer to Seymour than any other member of the family, and while he hardly seems well adjusted, he is less clearly psychotic than Seymour. Boo Boo first appears in the Glass saga as Boo Boo Tannenbaum, the mother of Lionel, the sensitive child hero of "Down at the Dinghy." In this story Salinger suggested the brutality of the world in the specific guise of anti-Semitism. Lionel has isolated himself from the world because he has overheard the family cook refer to his father as a "kike." Even though Lionel believes that a kike is " 'One of those things that go up in the air,' " he is horrified that his father should be considered such an obscurely unnatural phenomenon. Boo Boo's involvement with Zen Buddhism does not seem significant, and she is perhaps more down-to-earth than any of the other children, preferring to be thought of as a "Tuckahoe homemaker." Our only other encounter with Boo Boo is through the Sapphic scrawl which she leaves on a bathroom mirror on the day of Seymour's wedding: " 'Raise high the roof beam, carpenters. Like Ares comes the bridegroom, taller far than a tall man. Love, Irving Sappho, formerly under contract to Elysium Studios Ltd. Please be happy happy *happy* with your beautiful Muriel. This is an order. I outrank everybody on this block.' "

Of Waker we know no more than the fact that he has presumably found peace through becoming a Roman Catholic priest. In "Zooey," however, we learn that his answer offers no promise to the other children in the family. Walt never directly enters any of the Glass stories, although he seems to have certain qualities in common with an earlier Salinger creation, Sergeant Babe Gladwaller, the hero of "The Last Day of the Last Furlough" and the friend of Vincent Caulfield, Holden's older brother. We do learn, however, that Walt was killed in the Army of Occupation in Japan following the explosion of a Japanese stove which he was packing for his commanding officer. Walt is a symbol of innocence and tenderness for the heroine of "Uncle Wiggily in Connecticut." When she thinks of the innocence she has lost, Eloise has an alcoholic vision of the sophisticated squalor of her life and a moment of visionary love with her escapist daughter, Ramona. Eloise, who was once engaged to Walt, feels she has been destroyed by the exurbanite world her husband Lew represents (and when she refers to his favorite author as the unheard-of L. Manning Vines, she identifies him as the company commander who grudgingly gave Buddy leave to attend Seymour's wedding in "Raise High the Roof Beam, Carpenters"). Through the innocent love of a child Eloise achieves a moment of salvation similar to that which Sergeant X achieved, and, while like his salvation, hers is temporary and unstable, it nonetheless suggests the future development of Salinger's love theme.

When Salinger first introduces Franny Glass, she is a twenty-year-old college girl and summer-stock actress; and her older brother Zooey, who guides her through a religious crisis to the absurd love stance, is a television actor in his late twenties who suffers from an ulcer and, like Holden Caulfield, from profound disgust with the world of shams in which he lives. It is Zooey who gives the final *coup de grâce* to the idea of mysticism as an answer to the absurd universe.

"Franny" opens on a brilliantly lit Yale-game Saturday with Lane Coutell, Franny's date for the weekend (and her sometime lover, as we later learn), waiting on a railroad-station platform. He is rereading a letter from Franny which creates for the reader the impression of a typical college girl enthusiastically if somewhat vaguely in love. She hopes there will be an opportunity for dancing, that the weekend will not involve tiresome receiving lines, and that her spelling is improving. When Franny steps from the train the picture given by her letter seems to be elaborately confirmed:

> Franny was among the first of the girls to get off the train, from a car at the far, northern end of the platform. Lane spotted her immediately, and despite whatever it was he was trying to do with his face, his arm that shot up into the air was the whole truth. Franny saw it, and him, and waved extravagantly back. She was wearing a sheared raccoon coat, and Lane, walking toward her quickly but with a slow face, reasoned to himself, with suppressed excitement, that he was the only one who really *knew* Franny's coat. He remembered that once, in a borrowed car, after kissing Franny for a half hour or so, he had kissed her coat lapel, as though it were a perfectly desirable, organic extension of the person herself.

Lane pilots his date to a fashionable French restaurant, and it is only there that we see Franny as another of the Glass family suffering from "banana fever." She has begun to retreat into a world of mysticism, but like Seymour, she realizes the importance of an answer which will permit her to live in the real world. Her efforts at presenting a typical girl-on-a-football-weekend appearance are part of a last stand in which she tries to face the public world. Lane Coutell, the slick, falsely sophisticated representative of that world, is reminiscent of Muriel Fedders and her mother, and of Eloise's husband Lew. Franny is obviously on the verge of a nervous breakdown after a sudden depressing vision of the insignificance of the world around her that is emphasized by Lane's chatter about an "A" paper on Flaubert that he has written for a professor who lacks " 'testicularity.' " His chief interest in Franny rests in being seen with "an unimpeachably right-looking girl—a girl who was not only extraordinarily pretty but, so much the better, not too categorically cashmere sweater and flannel skirt."

In the beginning of the story Lane's own "phoniness" only encourages Franny to try more earnestly to fulfill the role he has outlined for her, but it gradually becomes clear that Franny suffers from an acute and oversensitive weariness with all that is phony in the world. Her mind wanders, and her lack of interest in Lane's distinctly "publishable" paper angers him. When he challenges her disinterestedness, she apologizes but adds that he is " 'talking just like a section man,' " and in her description of this Eastern-college phenomenon, Franny begins to outline her disillusionment.

When Lane interrupts her frenzied dissection of the junior faculty member Franny confesses not only that she has felt "*destructive*" all week, but that she had to strain to write the "natural" letter to him. Listening to Lane's description of the events of the weekend, Franny becomes progressively depressed and begins to ridicule Wally Campbell, the person giving the inevitable cocktail party. But Wally is only a symbol of Franny's disgust with those individuals who resign themselves to the phoniness of the world:

> "I don't mean there's anything horrible about him or anything like that. It's just that for four solid years I've kept seeing Wally Campbells wherever I go . . . It's *everybody*, I mean. Everything everybody does is so—I don't know—not *wrong*, or even mean, or even stupid necessarily. But just so tiny and meaningless and—sad-making. And the worst part is, if you go bohemian or something crazy like that, you're conforming just as much as everybody else, only in a different way."

Franny's description of her illness—or at least of one of its major manifestations—is reminiscent of Celia's description of her "perplexing" illness in T. S. Eliot's *The Cocktail Party*:

> An awareness of solitude.
> But that sounds so flat. I don't mean simply
> That there's been a crash: though indeed there has been.
> It isn't simply the end of an illusion
> In the ordinary way, or being ditched.
> Of course that's something that's always happening
> To all sorts of people, and they get over it
> More or less, or at least they carry on.
> No. I mean that what has happened has made me aware
> That I've always been alone. That one always is alone.
> Not simply the ending of one relationship,
> Not even simply finding that it never existed—
> But a revelation about my relationship
> With *everybody*. Do you know—
> It no longer seems worth while to *speak* to anyone!

Indeed, one of the first details we learn about Franny in "Zooey" is that, following her weekend with Lane, she no longer wants to speak to anyone.

The only thing that Franny can think of worth concerning herself over is something which interests Lane only superficially—a small, pea-green book entitled "The Way of a Pilgrim." The book has presumably been suggested to her by a professor, and she comes increasingly to see its message as her answer. When she almost loses control in the restaurant, she goes to the ladies' room and sits down with the book on her knees. "After a moment, she picked up the book, raised it chest-high, and pressed it to her—firmly, and quite briefly." The book seems momentarily to restore her control. The book which Franny clutches so zealously describes the search of a Russian peasant for the meaning of the biblical commandment to "pray incessantly." The peasant learns the solution from a "starets"—" 'some sort of terribly advanced religious person,' " who tells him to repeat the "Jesus Prayer" ("Lord Jesus Christ, have mercy on me") so often that the prayer becomes an automatic response of his heart. When the peasant has perfected his mystical prayer he walks all over Russia teaching people how to pray " 'by this incredible method.' " " 'He says,' " Franny adds, " 'that any name of God—any name at all—has this peculiar, self-active power of its own, and it starts working after you've sort of started it up.' " As Franny's excited description of the book continues, Lane's comments become as irrelevant (" 'I hate to mention it, but I'm going to reek of garlic' ") as the comments with which Franny had interrupted his discussion of Flaubert. Franny makes a final effort to adjust to Lane's idea of the "unimpeachably right-looking girl," but as she rises to leave, she faints, and when she awakens she is lying in a back room of the restaurant. The final satiric touch to Lane's insensitivity is given when he wonders if Franny does not simply need to go to bed with him.

"Zooey" begins on the Monday morning following Franny's weekend date with Lane; she has taken refuge on the couch in the Glass living room, where she clutches "The Way of a Pilgrim" and strokes the family cat, Bloomberg. Only two other members of the family are in the apartment, but the spirits of all the other brilliant Glass children crowd around Franny, "like so many Banquo's ghosts," threatening first to destroy her but suddenly offering her salvation. Just as Salinger warned us in "De Daumier-Smith's Blue Period" that he was not describing genuine mysticism, so he warns us in "Zooey" that what is to follow is not a mystical story but a love story which will take the form of a home movie (which in its close-ups, its attention to quotidian detail, and its casualness, it does). Pointing out that Nick Carraway in *The Great Gatsby* recognizes his cardinal virtue as his honesty, the narrator says, "*Mine*, I think, is that I know the difference between a mystical story and a love story. I say that my current offering isn't a mystical story, or a religiously mystifying story, at all. I say it's a compound, or multiple, love story, pure and complicated."

We are introduced to Zooey Glass at ten-thirty in the morning as he sits in "a very full bath" rereading a four-year-old letter from his brother Buddy. Among other things, the letter relates Buddy's arrival in Florida on the day following Seymour's suicide, but other than its value in filling in details in the ever-growing Glass legend, the letter from Buddy is important for the emphasis which it puts on the religious training which Franny and Zooey had received from their eldest brothers. Rather than urging the classics on the youngest children in the family, as they had urged them on the twins and Boo Boo, Buddy and Seymour decided to direct Franny and Zooey toward what is known in Zen as

"no-knowledge. Dr. Suzuki says somewhere that to be in a state of pure consciousness—*satori*—is to be with God before he said, Let there be light. Seymour and I thought that it might be a good thing to hold back this light from you and Franny (at least as far as we were able), and all the many lower, more fashionable lighting effects —the arts, sciences, classics, languages—till you were both able at least to conceive of a state of being where the mind knows the source of all light. We thought it would be wonderfully constructive to at least (that is, if our own 'limitations' got in the way) tell you as much as we knew about the men —the saints, the arhats, the bodhisattvas, the jivanmuktas—who knew something or everything about this state of being."

The description of this training for a state of pure consciousness is reinforced by a Taoist tale which Buddy (as narrator) repeats at the beginning of "Raise High the Roof Beam, Carpenters." The story had been read to Franny when she was an infant, but she always maintained that she could remember Seymour's reading it. In this brief Taoist allegory, Chiu-fang Kao has recently been retained by his Duke as a horse buyer, and he returns with the news that he has found a superlative horse—a dun-colored mare. When the animal turns out to be a coal-black stallion, the Duke is displeased, but his former horse-buyer exclaims with satisfaction,

"Has he really got as far as that? . . . Ah, then he is worth ten thousand of me put together. There is no comparison between us. What Kao keeps in view is the spiritual mechanism. In making sure of the essential, he forgets the homely details; intent on the inward qualities, he loses sight of the external. He sees what he wants to see, and not what he does not want to see. He looks at the things he ought to look at, and neglects those that need not be looked at. So

clever a judge of horses is Kao, that he has it in him to judge something better than horses."

Chiu-fang Kao had achieved the state of pure consciousness which Buddy and
Seymour envisioned for Franny and Zooey, and which Teddy McArdle possessed. Teddy's proposals represented Salinger's first consideration of Zen-
oriented education. Teddy believed that the first thing to be done with children
was to bring them together " 'and show them how to meditate.' " His primary
interest was in teaching children " 'who they *are*, not just what their names are
and things like that. . . . I'd get them to empty out everything their parents and
everybody ever told them. I mean even if their parents just told them an elephant's big, I'd make them empty *that* out. An elephant's big only when it's
next to something else—a dog or a lady, for example.' " If the children wanted
to learn other "stuff"—colors, names, categories—" 'they could do it, if they
felt like it, later on when they were older. But I'd want them to *begin* with all
the real ways of looking at things.' " Teddy's death prevents him from imple-
menting his scheme of education, but Franny and Zooey are the products of
controlled, intelligent experiments aimed at making them buyers who can always
distinguish a "superlative horse." Franny's crisis, like Zooey's cynicism, is a result
of this training, and her final victory is a throwing off of the banana fever of
Buddhism, which for all its beauty and hope, is not a solution for modern
Western man.

Zooey's private reverie over Buddy's letter is broken by the entrance of his
mother, and there follows a forty-seven-page dialogue in which we not only
glimpse Zooey's cynicism (toward television, the theatre, writers, almost anyone
who asks him to lunch), but also realize that beneath his cynical surface is a
strong core of love. His bantering attitude toward Bessie is largely a "routine"
which they have played so often that it is completely natural to them. Buddy
does not understand this attitude, and in his letter had somewhat patronizingly
requested, " 'Be kinder to Bessie, Zooey, when you can. I don't think I mean
because she's our mother, but because she's weary.' " At times Zooey's conversation with his mother seems no better integrated than Franny's conversation with
Lane, but his preoccupied manner is largely the result of his own efforts to
maintain an undistorted spiritual perspective. Bessie accuses Zooey of demon-
strating a family failing, an inability to be " 'any help when the chips are down.' "
He scoffs at the idea of being asked to live Franny's life for her, and especially at
the inevitable chicken broth Bessie offers as a cure-all. Bessie is right when she
says " 'You can't live in the world with such strong likes and dislikes,' " but she
does not realize that Zooey is coming to a realization about love which will not
only teach him that chicken broth is sacred, but will permit him to help Franny.

Buddy (who, symbolically, can never be reached in a crisis) offers no help with his mysticism; Waker, the Catholic priest, is out of the question because, as Zooey urges, " 'This thing with Franny is strictly non-sectarian;' " and Boo Boo is never considered.

Zooey makes the first important step toward relieving Franny's "fever" as well as his own when he realizes that "The Way of a Pilgrim" was not, as Franny told Lane, checked out of her school library, but was taken from the desk in Seymour and Buddy's old room. When he sees the pain which the mention of Seymour's name gives his mother, Zooey apologizes. "His apology had been genuine, and Mrs. Glass knew it, but evidently couldn't resist taking advantage of it, perhaps because of its rarity," to compare him unfavorably with Buddy. It is in his violent reaction to Bessie's reprimand that we first learn that Zooey is conscious of the sickness which he and Franny have inherited:

> "Buddy, Buddy, *Buddy*," he said. "Seymour, Seymour, *Seymour*."
> He had turned toward his mother, whom the crash of the razor had
> startled and alarmed but not really frightened. "I'm so sick of their
> names I could cut my throat." His face was pale but very nearly
> expressionless. "This whole goddam house stinks of ghosts. I don't
> mind so much being haunted by a dead ghost, but I resent like *hell*
> being haunted by a half-dead one. I wish to *God* Buddy'd make up
> his mind. He does everything else Seymour ever did—or tries to.
> Why the hell doesn't he kill himself and be done with it?"
> Mrs. Glass blinked her eyes, just once, and Zooey instantly looked
> away from her face. He bent over and fished his razor out of the
> wastebasket. "We're *freaks*, the two of us, Franny and I," he an-
> nounced, standing up. "I'm a twenty-five-year-old freak and she's a
> twenty-year-old freak, and both those bastards are responsible. . . .
> The symptoms are a little more delayed in Franny's case than mine,
> but she's a freak, too, and don't you forget it. I swear to you, I
> could murder them both without even batting an eyelash. The great
> teachers. The great emancipators. My God. I can't even sit down to
> lunch with a man any more and hold up my end of a decent conver-
> sation. I either get so bored or so goddam preachy that if the son of a
> bitch had any sense, he'd break his chair over my head."

When Zooey cites the fact that Franny's own symptoms are more "delayed" than his, we are able to see her revulsion and its crisis as a concentrated example of Zooey's own spiritual experience. Franny herself notes, after talking with Zooey from her couch-retreat, " 'We're not bothered by exactly the same things, but by the same kind of things, I think, and for the same reasons.' " In his efforts to bring Franny back into the world Zooey achieves final definition for his own struggle. Together they are able to scuttle out of the banana hole, achieving a victory important not only for its rejection of isolation but for its emphasis on participation in the world.

In arguing against Franny's withdrawal, Zooey emphasizes her misuse of the Jesus Prayer, for instead of resisting a world whose emphasis is on piling up " 'money, property, culture, knowledge, and so on and so on,' " she is attempting to pile up another kind of treasure, less material, but just as negotiable. " 'Ninety per cent of all the world-hating saints in history,' " Zooey argues, " 'were just as acquisitive and unattractive, basically, as the rest of us are.' " Because he was brought up on the same perfectionist principles, Zooey understands Franny's mystical retreat from the world and her hope for some kind of miracle that will provide salvation. Her insistence on a mystical salvation, however, is only another example of the way in which they have been " 'side-tracked. Always, always, always referring every goddam thing that happens back to our lousy little egos.' " Zooey does not oppose the Jesus prayer itself so much as "why and how and *where*" Franny is using it. Franny is not fulfilling any duty in life through the prayer but merely substituting it for her real duty. It is this fatal tendency to leave the realities of life behind which makes Franny and Zooey "freaks." " 'You don't face any facts. This same damned attitude of not facing facts is what got you into this messy state of mind in the first place, and it can't possibly get you out of it.' " If Christ has a real function, it is not to take man up in his arms and relieve him of all his duties and make all his "nasty *Weltschmerzen*" go away.

In her dedication to the Jesus Prayer Franny has tried to make what Albert Camus regarded as the suicidal leap into faith. Franny's real crisis is not the result of the fact that she has reached an acute depth of despair, but that she is on the brink of becoming, like Seymour, a misfit who can never accept or be accepted by society. Franny is consequently in danger of joining the other Salinger heroes who refuse to come to terms with reality, confusing the life of isolation with the life of the spirit. Despite his disgust with stereotyped scripts and the "phonies" with whom he is so often cast, Zooey has fought to maintain a contact with reality. His realization of the danger of fleeing to the deceptive private world gives him an insight which the rest of the family lacks, and hence he is the only member to have forgiven Seymour his suicide because he is the only one who fully understands it. So anxious is Zooey to maintain his contact with reality—however painful it may be—that he is hesitant about the idea of going to Paris to make a movie. Any movement away from the specific world in which he has suffered seems distinctly suspect. To Franny the idea of making a movie in Paris is exciting, but Zooey counters her,

"It is not exciting. That's exactly the point. I'd enjoy doing it, yes. *God*, yes. But I'd hate like hell to leave New York. . . . I was *born* here. I went to *school* here. I've been *run over* here—twice, and on the same damn *street*. I have no business acting in Europe, for God's sake."

After trying unsuccessfully to convince Franny that the Jesus Prayer offers her no answer, Zooey enters Seymour and Buddy's old room. Picking up the phone still listed in Seymour's name, Zooey calls his sister and, disguising his voice, pretends to be Buddy. This is not the call from Seymour which Franny had said she wanted, but Buddy is so much the dead man's spiritual counterpart that there is little difference. Although Zooey's impersonation finally rings false, he has captured Franny's attention, and she is more prepared to listen than she was when he stretched out on the living room floor and lectured her. The absurd vision which Zooey is finally able to impart to Franny is that everything in the world, no matter how base or corrupt, is sacred. Salinger has continually reiterated the fact that "reality" has presented both young people impressions of deceit, pettiness, and insensitivity. The intention to see the world as sacred is, therefore, in total opposition to reality and a profound example of metaphysical absurdity. Until she adopts this vision, Zooey argues, she will never have the religious satisfaction she craves: " 'You don't even have enough sense to *drink* when somebody brings you a cup of consecrated chicken soup—which is the only kind of chicken soup Bessie ever brings to anybody around this madhouse.' " Franny begins to be persuaded when Zooey argues that

> "The only thing you can do now, the only re*li*gious thing you can do, is *act*. Act for God, if you want to—be *God's* actress, if you want to. . . . One other thing. And that's all. I promise you. But the thing is, you raved and bitched . . . about the stupidity of audiences. The goddam 'unskilled laughter' coming from the fifth row. And that's right, that's right—God knows it's depressing. I'm not saying it isn't. But that's none of your business, really. That's none of your business, Franny. An artist's only concern is to shoot for some kind of perfection, and *on his own terms*, not anyone else's. You have no right to think about those things, I swear to you. Not in any real sense, anyway. You know what I mean?"

Franny's realization—and now also Zooey's own—can come through dedication to her art. Camus saw art as the most complete and successful form of rebellion, since the artist reconstructs the world according to his own plan (his concern "to shoot for some kind of perfection"). "Art is the activity that exalts and denies simultaneously," and it therefore "should give us a final perspective on the content of rebellion." While Camus agrees with Nietzsche's dictum that

" 'No artist tolerates reality,' " he also argues that "no artist can get along with-out reality." A lack of toleration and an escape are two different things; "art disputes reality, but does not hide from it." Nietzsche had argued that all forms of transcendence were slanders against this world and against life, but Camus envisions a nonsupernatural but "living transcendence, of which beauty carries the promise, which can make this mortal and limited world preferable to and more appealing than any other. Art thus leads us back to the origins of rebellion to the extent that it tries to give its form to an elusive value which the future perpetually promises, but of which the artist has a presentiment and wishes to snatch from the grasp of history." Art is a paramount quixotic gesture by which man attempts to give order (at least an order in the same sense of making statements about individual experience or a state of being) to a disordered world. In support of his arguments, Camus cites Van Gogh's complaint as "the arrogant and desperate cry of all artists. 'I can very well, in life and in painting, too, do without God. But I cannot, suffering as I do, do without something that is greater than I am, that is my life—the power to create.' "

Zooey has shown his tormented sister the absurd gesture which she can make, and suggests that in making it she will not only affirm her intention to find order and meaning in life, but also realize the goal of "The Wise Child," whose obligation it is both to know and be himself. Franny recognizes the validity of this gesture, but Zooey goes on to infuse her with the absurd belief that will give the gesture its final meaning. He recalls that when as a child he had rebelled against having to polish his shoes for the "moronic" audience and spon-sors of "It's a Wise Child," Seymour had taken him aside and asked him to shine them for the Fat Lady. " 'He never did tell me who the Fat Lady was, but I shined my shoes for the Fat Lady every time I ever went on the air again.' " Zooey always pictured Seymour's Fat Lady sitting on her porch listening to the radio, swatting flies, and dying of cancer. He then learns that Seymour had once told Franny to be funny for the Fat Lady, and the blaring radio and cancer were part of the fantasy Franny had created just as they were part of Zooey's. In the final moments of this "pure and complicated love story," Zooey explains the Fat Lady's identity:

> "I don't care where an actor acts. It can be in summer stock, it can be over the radio, it can be over *tele*vision, it can be in a goddam Broadway theatre, complete with the most fashionable, most well-fed, most sunburned-looking audience you can imagine. But I'll tell you a terrible secret—Are you listening to me? *There isn't anyone out there who isn't Seymour's Fat Lady.* That includes your Pro-fessor Tupper, buddy. And all his goddam cousins by the dozens.

There isn't anyone *any*where who isn't Seymour's Fat Lady. Don't
you know that? Don't you know that goddam secret yet? And don't
you know—*listen* to me now—*don't you know who that Fat Lady
really is?* . . . Ah, buddy. Ah, buddy. It's Christ Himself. Christ
Himself, buddy."

For a moment all Franny can do—"for joy, apparently"—is cradle the
phone in her hands, but at the conclusion of the story she falls "into a deep,
dreamless sleep," like the sleep of Sergeant X in "For Esmé—with Love and
Squalor." While neither mysticism nor religion in its traditional sense "provides
an answer to the search of any of the members of the Glass family, a concern for
mystic and religious experience provides a path to Zooey's and Franny's conception of perfect love. . . . That conception includes, embraces, and goes beyond
the ordinary conceptions of religion and morality (and in its humanness, stops
short of mysticism) and can properly be called by no other name than the simple
and profound name of love." To love the mercenaries, the butchers, the deceivers,
the phonies of the world with the idea that each of them is Christ is to assume a
preponderantly absurd stance. Zooey's message is not to love man as Christ
would have loved him, but to love man *as* Christ. There is no appeal to a final
supernatural authority, no desire for mystical transcendence, no hope that a better
world awaits man as a reward for his struggle. Zooey is at last able to convince
Franny that, as Sherwood Anderson's Dr. Parcival stated, "everyone in the world
is Christ and they are all crucified."

[To act with morality and love in a universe in which God is dead (or, at
least, in which historical preconceptions of God frequently seem invalid) is perhaps the most acute problem of our age. Salinger's intense consideration of that
problem in large part accounts for the fact that, while he is one of the least
prolific authors writing today, he is the most popular. The progression from
early stories in which the misfit hero can find genuine love only in children to the
later stories in which mysticism is rejected in favor of an absurd love stance is a
progression whose scope is perhaps not fully measured in the stories which
Salinger has written, but more specifically in the personal struggle he has under-
gone in arriving at this philosophical position/ There is no question that the
author loves Seymour, and it is with an uneasy feeling that the reader is compelled to reject this Christ-like man. Salinger began the Glass saga with Seymour's suicide, and since that time has been writing his way around and back to
that day in 1945 in order to show where Seymour failed. Seymour is at least
partly exonerated for making "freaks" of Franny and Zooey when we note that
it was his death (and its admission of failure) which saved the youngest Glass
children; in a metaphorical sense in no way foreign to Salinger's intention, Sey-

mour (who could, in fact, *see more* than his contemporaries) died that Franny and Zooey might live, and it is in this sense of his almost ritualistic death, rather than in the deluding mysticism of his life, that one seizes on the essence of this character's saintliness. Through Seymour's death, Zooey learns that the Fat Lady, the eternal vulgarian, must not be passed over for any mystical discipline. As Ihab Hassan has observed, "Zooey's message constitutes high praise of life. It is the sound of humility, calling us to *this* world. The vulgarian and the outsider are reconciled, not in the momentary flash of a quixotic gesture, nor even in the exclusive heart of a mystical revelation, but in the constancy of love." And in this light it can, no doubt, be safely conjectured that "the sound of one hand clapping" is precisely, triumphantly, the commonplace sound of the Fat Lady swatting flies.

MAX F. SCHULZ

Epilogue to "Seymour: An Introduction": Salinger and the Crisis of Consciousness

Salinger's imagination has begun to impose upon the reader. Like the initialed mystery of his name and the childish nicknames of the Glass children, his prose nowadays darkens more than illuminates, obscures more than enlightens. Despite the steady maturing of an incredibly skillful technique, Salinger finds himself writing words that multiply fractionally, so that more and more adds up to less and less. The paradox is that he seeks greater depths of communication. Unfinished dialogue, telephone conversations, letters, diaries, and bathroom mirror messages are brilliantly manipulated within the linear limitations of the print-bound media to approximate what Marshall McLuhan calls the immediacy and disjunction of the new electronic media and what Salinger would define as the comprehensiveness and simultaneity of the Zen visionary experience. Contrariwise, this strategy of Salinger's language also images, inadvertently, a breakdown of communication in our century (in spite of the paper blizzard, or, if McLuhan is right, because of it), for the unfinished, disjointed, and cut-up dialogues of his characters reflect the retreat of mechanized mass man into indirect articulation. Salinger's exploration of the spiritual ways in which man's sensibility can reach out to touch another's has become paradoxically a rendering of the incommunication intrinsic to the modern scene. Most intriguing in this reversal of situations is that in *The Catcher in the Rye* and the stories chronicling the Glass family, Salinger has become less and less a recorder of the phenomenon and increasingly a mute testifier to its truth. His receptivity to this distinctly modern problem mirrors a crisis of consciousness in J. D. *Buddy*frannyzooeyseymour–Salinger, whose exacerbated sensibility seems to be reflecting ever multiple refractions of

From *Studies in Short Fiction* 5, no. 2 (Winter 1968). © 1967 by Newberry College.

reality, with infinity apparently the end in mind. Since Buddy is of all the Glasses the most complete spokesman for Salinger (the blurring of the two identities has reached the point where Buddy has laid claim to Salinger's one novel and four of his short stories), "Seymour: An Introduction," which is Buddy's most ambitious creative effort to date (at least that we have been shown), is probably the best work to examine for clues to the imaginative impasse which I believe to be presently troubling Salinger.

Stanley Edgar Hyman comments angrily in a review of Salinger that the Glass series has progressed in little more than one decade from one of the finest short stories of our time, "A Perfect Day for Bananafish," to one of the most appalling ever written, "Seymour: An Introduction." He applauds Salinger's steady drift away from the well-made story of the New Yorker into the ever widening pool of experience; but, he carps, a maturing writer breaks through limiting forms into fuller and deeper form, such as those of Moby-Dick or Ulysses, not into anarchy and incoherence. "Seymour: An Introduction" is not, however, without its defenders. John O. Lyons contends that Salinger has resuscitated the effective literary stance of the early nineteenth-century romantics, whose experience presupposed (1) the mysterious interrelation of things, with the identification of art and reality, and (2) the writer as the subject of his art, with form in endless process, not a completed product, of creation. Joseph L. Blotner (in the same issue of WSCL) would consign Salinger to an even earlier literary epoch, asserting that Buddy's "interminable, reminiscent colloquy with the reader" represents a fictional study in "something like hysteria" and that if Salinger continues this mode of the anti-short story far enough he will be writing "something very like Aubrey's Brief Lives or the Conversations of William Drummond of Hawthorndon." Henry Anatole Grunwald in the introduction to his edition of Salinger criticism argues along somewhat the same lines that Salinger is concerned not so much with a characterization of Seymour as with pulling off an indirect revelation of Buddy's personality. And Ihab Hassan contends that Salinger is engaged in the risky experiment of constructing stories that will convey through form a sacramental view of life and through language the Zen ideal of the silence of things espoused by Seymour and his disciple Buddy. Rather than attempt still another rhetorical exegesis of the astonishing direction that Salinger's muse has taken, I wish to approach this question of Buddy's wordiness as posing for Salinger a problem in point of view that is, in origin at least, more psycho-religious than literary. Indeed, one needs to emphasize this point. We cannot in any final critical judgment separate the religious and artistic intentions in Salinger's work.

Buddy as portrayed in "Seymour: An Introduction" is a man wracked by contradictions. He presents the anomaly of a Zen enthusiast in retreat from sensation and of a creative mind in unmediated contact with the world. He is "a species of literary shut-in," living alone in a "cringing, little house" (surely a trope for his sensibility), "set deep in the woods and on the more inaccessible side of a mountain," where he sees "very few people during the working week or year." Despite this refinement of surroundings for contemplation, his portrait of Seymour remains unformulated and incomplete, because he cannot discriminate among his memories. "It would help enormously," he cries forlornly, "if some kind soul were to send me a telegram stating precisely which Seymour he'd prefer me to describe." When Buddy tries to characterize Seymour, he gets "a vivid-type picture" of Seymour "simultaneously at the ages of approximately eight, eighteen, and twenty-eight, with a full head of hair and getting very bald, wearing a summer camper's red-striped shorts and wearing a creased suntan shirt with buck-sergeant stripes, sitting in padmasana and sitting in the balcony at the R. K. O. 86th street." In short, the whole stream of experience impinges on his sensibility. Like Seymour's face ("the last absolutely unguarded adult face in the Greater New York Area"), Buddy's sensibility has no built-in defenses. It responds to *all* stimuli, swelling into "a thesaurus of undetached prefatory remarks." When he narrates an incident about Seymour, irrelevant, minor, and insignificant details jostle each other in noisy clamor to gain his harried attention. A reminiscence of Seymour's answer to an innocuous question put by their father, Les, balloons with expanding surface: instantly Buddy recalls "Seymour, sitting in an old corduroy armchair across the room, a cigarette going, wearing a blue shirt, gray slacks, moccasins with the counters broken down, a shaving cut on the side of his face that I could see." Hence Buddy's near breakdown in communication when he gives up trying "for Selectiveness with a description" ("I can't sort out," he laments, "can't clerk with this man") and, engulfed in particulars, begins to give us Seymour, hair by hair, and ears by eyes by nose by skin to get at the face. Seymour has become "much too large to fit on ordinary typewriter paper," he confesses, ostensibly paying tribute to his brother's larger-than-life saintliness but also betraying his own unmediating sensibility. Buddy is the victim of what Coleridge and Wordsworth a century and a half ago recognized epistemologically as a despotism of the senses, which destroys one's self-identity and hence one's imaginative control of experience.

Understandably Buddy's effort to reduce his memories to esthetic form leaves him exhausted and even physically ill. A "little pentimento" about Seymour's instruction in how to shoot marbles starts him "sweating literally from head to foot." The description of Seymour's nose, he tells himself, will "only hurt a minute." The subject of Seymour's ears causes his hands to sweat and his bowels to churn. "The Integrated Man is simply not at home" he laments. And after recalling the show-business environment of his childhood, he suffers an attack of hepatitis. But again the anomaly. Not frustration but joy puts him on the sick list. "Professionally speaking," he confesses at the outset, "I'm an ecstatically happy man." Still, he admits, "an ecstatically happy writing person is often a totally draining type to have around." Moreover he is prone to self-immolation. The "true artist-seer" is "dazzled to death by . . . the blinding shapes and colors of his own sacred human conscience." If a pun on *consciousness* is not intended here, certainly the persistent pressure of Buddy's "confession" in the story makes it eminently applicable. For the writer and man of unmediated sensation, then, personal happiness—joy—becomes identifiable, as Buddy in a hesitant side step admits, with liverishness. Openness of the senses, aliveness of the spirit, is akin to inflammation of the organs. No wonder Buddy believes that Seymour, an *echte Dichter*, carried "the Muse of Absolute Joy" on his back like the monkey of addiction and that Beethoven increased and improved in creativity "after he ceased being encumbered with a sense of hearing."

The joy Buddy has in mind here is concomitant with the Zen ideal of *satori*, "to be in a state of pure consciousness" (so he defines it, quoting Dr. Suzuki, in a letter to Zooey), of the flow of things in the universe. In such a comprehension of the natural way of things, self-effacement paradoxically is not involved, because self does not exist. In fact, the comprehension *is* that there is no self. Hence one is reinstated in the natural flow without the artificial barrier of a sense of otherness. The experience is clearly akin to the "spots of time" in Wordsworth's life when the external world ceased to exist for him apart from the image of that world in his mind. Why then the illness? Both Seymour and Buddy are writers as well as Zen neophytes; and literature and Zen—despite the cosmic paradox of such great Chinese Taoist poets as Chuang-tzu—seek irreconcilable goals. Seymour, the holy guru as bananafish, gorged himself on sensation in an effort to achieve nirvana. Buddy wishes to emulate Seymour in the same religious gesture at indiscriminate love of all things. Yet he also nervously wishes to practice the highly discriminating art of writing, which we learn from Seymour is also Buddy's religion. The two gestures, contrary to Seymour's tendency to confuse them, are incompatible, the one a private apprehension of being, the other a public rendering of objects. Even Wordsworth, whose greatness as a poet lies, in part, in his ability to communicate his experience esthetically, kept the two separate in his mind. If, for him, at moments of identification with nature, as he tells us in *The Prelude*,

> the light of sense
> Goes out, but with a flash that has revealed
> The invisible world,

like an enormous short-circuiting of perception brought on by an overload of the senses with the world of objects, still his poetic rendering of the experience *selectively* invokes the visible world. Buddy's problem is his failure in straining for communicable form to keep these contradictory impulses separate.

One may start from another angle, Buddy's likeness to Seymour, and one will arrive at the same broken sentence and blank sheet of paper. To Buddy, a junior tagging after his brilliant two-years older brother, Seymour (who represented "all *real* things" to the other Glass children) was an ideal to be jealously, despairingly emulated. Seymour was the tireless person who made Buddy the "Second-Fastest Boy Runner in the World," who played inimitable stoopball superior to any kid in the neighborhood and demon-inspired games of Ping-Pong and football, and who was "*never* wrong." The similarity of the two brothers, as contrasted to the four younger Glass children, is physical as well. Their noses and lack of chins were "close to being identical." Buddy unwittingly reveals his subconscious desires, when, in alluding to his story about Seymour's suicide ("A Perfect Day for Bananafish"), he admits to having described "the young man, the 'Seymour,' who did the walking and talking . . . not to mention the shooting," not after Seymour but "oddly" after "someone with a striking resemblance to—alley oop, I'm afraid-myself." In a backhanded fashion in one of his parenthetical disclosures, Buddy later acknowledges that his efforts at a description of Seymour involve his own ego, his "perpetual lust to share top billing" with his older brother. Hence the act of recreating Seymour becomes for Buddy an endless, terrifying exploration into himself. In this respect Buddy is a true romantic and "Seymour: An Introduction" as romantic a work as Byron's *Don Juan* or Wordsworth's *The Prelude*. "I *yearn* to talk, to be queried, to be interrogated, about this particular dead man," he exclaims; but he cannot enjoy being his "brother's brother for nothing." The price he must pay is personal discovery. Each scrap of fact about Seymour has attached to it a revelation about Buddy. It is this note of the *intime* that the baffled Buddy is "really not up to." At the beginning of his attempt to write about Seymour, he distinguishes between professional speech and private speech. The one is a joyous exercise, the other a sweaty penance. His trouble is that the story of Seymour blurs the two activities. Hence his inability to get on with the tale and his envy of the reader's "golden silence." He stalls with ballooning details about Seymour. The "drama of reason," Coleridge once called the luxuriant spread of parenthetical expressions in his prose, that presents "the thought growing, instead of a mere Hortus siccus"; and Buddy echoes him in tagging his "early [and late]-blooming parentheses" "the bowlegged—buckle-legged—omens of my state of mind and body at this writing." Understandably his "psychedelic" backings and forwardings into the times of his and Seymour's selves end in sweaty silence—or, the same thing, in hepatitis, Buddy's inventive variation on bananafish gorging. Like Seymour, he can utter "cries for help" at intervals, only to "decline to say in perfectly intelligible language where it hurt" at length.

But what of Salinger? In the fictional charade of the Glass family, Seymour functions as surrogate of Buddy and Buddy as alter ego of Salinger. That much is evident. Less evident are the implications to date and for his future in this literary ploy of a tale about a pseudonymous alter ego's surrogate, which pretends at once to distance the author from and to merge him with the flow of experience. "Seymour: An Introduction" represents in its portrait of Buddy a skillful dramatization of a creative mind at the crossroads, in agony over the spiritual problem of how to travel simultaneously the bisecting roads of the actual and the ideal that meet somewhere between this and the next world and between oneself and another man's being. That is certainly an ethical theme that this and the other Glass stories explore, but there are also important considerations about creativity implied in the rendering of the theme. (If this assumption confuses the author with his fictional creation, then the author himself must be indicted along with me as an accessory.) The writing of "Seymour: An Introduction," with its attempt to create a modern saint, images an unbearably paralyzed ambience of the creative spirit. It retails *sub rosa* a terrifying confession of the havoc wrought in the romantic mind when it grapples in isolation with inchoate raw experience. One is reminded of the din, the painful bellowing and energetic despair, of the efforts of Los, Blake's personification of the imagination, to give form to matter. One cannot easily forget that the fires of Los's energy eventually burn out and Los lies inert, frozen, in the "nerveless silence" of "a cold solitude and dark void," foreshadowing Blake's own verbal silence the last twenty years of his life.

The signs in Salinger's work are similarly there for one to read. Buddy–Salinger admires Seymour's poems for their impersonality. The more autobiographical they "appear to be, or *are*, the less revealing the content is of any known details of his actual daily life in this Western world." They fulfill the ideal of Zen, revealing emotion and personality without "spilling a single really autobiographical bean." That is to say, when Seymour is least "personal," least involved with "self" (since ego according to Zen is purely illusion), he is most truthful. It is not entirely coincidental that all the Glasses have more than a touch of the actor in them, another way of achieving this ideal. But Buddy significantly is less the poet-mystic than Seymour and less the actor than Franny or Zooey. Like Salinger he is a storyteller; "Seymour: An Introduction" is his sprawling prose effort to emulate his brother's achievement. Interestingly, however, he produces the exact reverse of Seymour's double haikus. Prodigally he distributes autobiographical beans about on the page, ignoring the niceties of literary expression in his frenzy to realize the *koan*-like wholeness of Seymour. In short, a persona has not helped Salinger to achieve the distance necessary for imposing imaginative form on experience. He identifies as closely with Buddy as Buddy with Seymour, and Seymour is committed to the Taoist goal of indiscriminate embrace of the world. Few men's nervous systems have the appetite for such a program and few artists the synthesizing powers for such a task. Buddy–Salinger seems to comprehend this; yet, like the old vaudeville team of Gallagher and Glass, he finds himself unable or unwilling to update his routine. As early as *The Catcher in the Rye*, Buddy–Salinger's most impersonal and still most successful book, even though and perhaps in part because least ambitious, Holden Caulfield is made to reject the careful selectiveness of Hemingway's manner as phony. A thorough romantic Buddy–Salinger will embrace all experience—*or none.*

The ambivalence of that aim appears everywhere in his stories. "Don't ever tell anybody anything," Holden warns the reader. "If you do, you start missing everybody." His ideal of a future is to pretend to be a deaf-mute married to a real deaf-mute. "Then I'd be through with having conversations for the rest of my life," he thinks, adding details to his fantasy that unmistakably parallel Buddy's real-life situation: "Everybody'd think I was just a poor deaf-mute bastard and they'd leave me alone . . . and I'd build me a little cabin somewhere . . . and live there for the rest of my life." Yet, although he does not tell his "whole goddam autobiography," he does spill *all* "about this madman stuff." In "Raise High the Roof Beam, Carpenters," Seymour summarizes in his diary a conversation he had with the analyst of his fiancée's mother: "I told him . . . [apropos of the Gettysburg Address] that 51,112 men were casualties at Gettysburg, and that if someone *had* to speak at the anniversary of the event, he should simply have come forward and shaken his fist at this audience and then walked off—that is, if the speaker was an absolutely honest man." In further discussion with the analyst about his being a perfectionist, Seymour takes to the hustings in favor of indiscriminate experience, "on the ground that it leads to health and a kind of very real, enviable happiness," even though he recognizes that "for a discriminating man to achieve this . . . he would have to dispossess himself of poetry, go *beyond* poetry. That is, he couldn't possibly learn or drive himself to *like* bad poetry in the abstract, let alone equate it with good poetry. He would have to drop poetry altogether." Here the indiscriminate embrace of all experience leads inevitably to the Taoist's silence. One of the still unanswered mysteries about Seymour is why his loving absorption of all life became nihilistic for him, ending in his suicide. As a poet, could he have mistakenly confused verbal silence with personal nihilism? Whatever the illogic of his act, it inadvertently substantiates Cadmium Greene's rhetorical question (in Earl Rovit's novel *The Player King*) about whether "the pathetic yen for Zen" is not one of the "sickly suicides" of our time—"the deceptively buoyant bubble of air in the veins." In the climax of "A Perfect Day for Bananafish" Buddy–Salinger does not shrink from the integrity of the artistic act. To unite with all life indiscriminately is to deny any immediate object of one's love. As Seymour's mother-in-law is reported in "Raise High the Roof Beam, Carpenters" to have said, Seymour has "never learned to relate to anybody." The net effect of Franny's step from squalor toward love at the end of "Zooey" is similar. When Zooey hangs up the telephone after telling her about Seymour's parable of the Fat Lady who is Christ, for whom he used to shine his shoes before going on the radio, "Franny took in her breath slightly but continued to hold the phone to her ear. A dial tone, of course, followed the formal break in the connection. She appeared to find it extraordinarily beautiful to listen to, rather as if it were the best possible substitute for the primordial silence itself." The heroic effort, to date, of Salinger to portray the Glass children's flirtation with religious enlightenment—willy nilly Buddhist or Christian (why not Judaic?)—by way of telling *all* about them constantly threatens to end in the same stellar nothingness or in its complement, the cancerous formlessness of the recent stories. His meld with Buddy has not altered but rather intensified this problem. For Buddy to achieve satori is for Salinger to court a nullification potentially disastrous for writing; whereas for Buddy to fall short of enlightenment is for Salinger to develop a psychological theme other than a paean to the attainment of the full spiritual life in America.

Nothing in Salinger's latest story, "Hapworth 16, 1924," published six years after "Seymour: An Introduction," refutes these conclusions. Buddy has lapsed into silence. As a substitute, however, he has finally screwed up his courage sufficiently to let us look at one of Seymour's writings: in the words of Seymour a "very long, boring letter" written "at blissful random," more inchoate in structure and cute in tone than any of the stories that preceded it. Salinger has dispensed with the alter ego of Buddy—who at least pretended to some of the ordering instincts of a writer of fiction but who is here reduced to the ineffectual role of copiest—and succumbed to the self-indulgence of the seven-year-old Seymour's account in a letter to the folks back home of his and Buddy's happenings at a summer camp in Maine.

The by now familiar obsession of Seymour—even at seven—is only too evident. "It is not in your son Buddy's nature or mine or your son Walter's to be in the least shocked or disgusted by any sweet, earthly side of humankind," he tells his mother and father. "Indeed, *all* [that key word again] forms of human folly and bestiality touch a very sympathetic chord within our breasts!" Even, he assures them, the beautiful, "despised, touching pimples," blemishes, and cysts on human bodies. Not even sibling rivalry upsets Seymour's euphoria. He is full of schoolgirl praise of that "droll and thrilling companion," that "dear, comical," "maddening, indomitable" younger brother of his, the "most resourceful creation of God." He quotes Blake's Proverb of Hell, "Damn braces, bless relaxes," and proudly assures Les and Bess that he and five-year-old Buddy are "damning braces all over the place"—most visibly in the unfettered renderings of this letter. He even declines anesthesia for eleven stitches in his leg because he will not give up his state of consciousness for flimsy reasons. And his passion for sanctifying all experiences prompts him to by-pass Caruso in favor of Mr. Bubbles, of Buck and Bubbles, "merely singing softly to himself in his dressing room" in Cleveland. The same indiscriminate appetite has him reading all the books on God or merely religious from A to Z, all books in the public library on the structure of the human heart and on the formation of the callus, and all the back comic strips of Moon Mullins.

Some idea of the rambling sprawl of the story is suggested by the list of books Seymour asks to be sent to him. It occupies—with gratuitous interspersed remarks, again "at random," about Charlotte Brontë's carnal attractions and other such "insights" of a seven-year-old genius into the authors he is reading—one fourth of the letter! Buddy–Salinger's resort to the letter of a seven-year-old is a resourceful tactic for giving credence and inevitability, if not esthetic responsibility, to such insouciant dips into the pool of experience. But the trick does not hide the growing desperation of this reliance on the mouths of little babes. The child as saint grows somewhat stale in repetition—and quite suspicious when, as in this case, he is merely a ventriloquistic device for the voice and thoughts of the author. Hyman's estimate following publication of "Seymour: An Introduction" of the cul-de-sac Salinger has gotten himself into still holds true. "His highway has turned into a dirt road, then into wagon ruts, finally into a squirrel track and climbed a tree." From his treetop only the great, empty sky unfolds in primordial quiet. It would seem that the ambiguity of the Glass name as metaphor has its insidious consequences. It is not accidental that Buddy-frannyzooeyseymour are Glasses, bent on not just the myope's refracted *aperçus* of the bay but on the mystic's wide-eyed vision of the world, a luminous purchase on eternity. Given Salinger's proclivity for a dramatic frame in his Glass stories, he may find the way down from his tree and back onto the highway with the prosaic eyes of one of the non-Zen Glasses, whose point of view has not yet been explored. Surely Gallagher and Glass offer Salinger's religious mystique few of the temptations to identify with them as have their progeny. If their outlook is not the route to spiritual salvation, it may prove the turn to esthetic redemption, for they too are artists of a sort, with a practical idea of what does not "go" with audiences. Or will it? After all, Les and Bess sired and spawned the brood and must have some of the aspirations of their children lodged in their own chromosomes. It may well be that his obsessive creation of the Glasses was a wrong move for Salinger and he will never be able to achieve with them, in the words of Ihab Hassan, "the forms of dramatic permanence."

HELEN WEINBERG

J. D. Salinger's Holden and Seymour and the Spiritual Activist Hero

Mary McCarthy attacks J. D. Salinger's work as sentimental and narcissistic. One expects coolheadedness, tough-mindedness, from Miss McCarthy, and this is of course what she is giving her reader in assailing Salinger's sentimentality; but her view of his narcissism is not tough-minded. To criticize Salinger's work on psychological rather than literary grounds seems to me too arbitrary and simpleminded a method of judging his representation of reality. And it is on psychological grounds that Miss McCarthy's case against Salinger's oral-anal narcissism finally rests. As such it gives us a valid footnote on the Salinger hero but not, I think, a valid or full criticism of him. It would be a narrow psychology which did not make reference to the oral-anal narcissism possible in man; it would be a narrow literature, indeed, which had for its only hero the fully genital hero of Wilhelm Reich and D. H. Lawrence.

On the other hand, other critics of Salinger overemphasize the Freudian validity of his insights. Gwynn and Blotner's book, while useful for its bibliography and general comment, is clumsy in its Freudian analysis of some of the stories. In "De Daumier-Smith's Blue Period," for example, it does the most shocking job of Freudian analysis possible in its insistence on the castration complex as centrally significant in that story. Blotner, Mary McCarthy, and all those who talk about Salinger's works as if they were case histories forget that we are all post-Freudian: Salinger, too, is post-Freudian, and to analyze him for his readers in Freudian terms is meaningless.

Facile Freudian criticism of modern literature is no longer possible. Perhaps

From *The New Novel in America: The Kafkan Mode in Contemporary Fiction.* © 1970 by Cornell University. Cornell University Press, 1970.

Freud's insights clarify great literary intuitions of the past. We may realize Hamlet's situation to a fuller extent if Hamlet is seen in the light of the Oedipal complex. However, today's literature is post-Freudian: it starts from Freud; it includes Freud; it leaps out of and away from Freud; it opposes itself to Freudian clichés along with a host of other sorts of inherited clichés. The post-Freudian novelist has been given what the post-Freudian critic or reader has been given. I think a modern novelist expects the reader to assume the Freudian ideas with him as part of the general intelligence which he brings to bear on (or which he opposes to) the reality that he presents in his novel.

It is, in fact, on the basis of the recognition that the investigation of heroes with wonderfully varied psyches and an assortment of psychological differences which remain outside Freudian (or other established psychological) categories is possible in literature that I would find fault with much of the favorable and unfavorable criticism of Salinger. Salinger, as many new novelists do, explores possibilities outside normal behavior and outside the usual categories for abnormal behavior. Clearly, today's novelists are not psychological realists in any of the established ways.

However, Salinger may attract critiques based on psychological categorizing from his admirers and detractors because he cheats, especially in his earlier work, on his own vision (a vision of goodness on the edge of madness) in order to structure a story according to external, formalized rules of the storytelling craft. I am not talking of the twenty stories of the apprentice period; these are experiments in storytelling in a number of styles: the styles of F. Scott Fitzgerald, Katherine Mansfield, and a little of the simple surprise-ending stuff of O. Henry. Nor do I find a conflict between vision and form in seven of the *Nine Stories*. All except "Teddy" and "De Daumier-Smith's Blue Period" are formal studies of love and loneliness; all have the *New Yorker* tone as they make their understatements on the sweet and the sad in modern life. They are, no matter how successful of their kind (in the way, for example, that "For Esmé—with Love and Squalor" is successful), slight and ephemeral. They are informed by no special vision. "Teddy" and "De Daumier-Smith" are informed by a mystical vision of madness which provides the way to fullness of being otherwise unavailable in modern life. The vision in these two stories is just beginning to be defined and is, therefore, only contained in some conceptual form within the confines of the craftsmanlike story—the vision is not strong enough to conflict with the form or insist upon a form of its own. In *The Catcher in the Rye* the vision conflicts with the tight formalistic planning; in "Seymour: An Introduction," the vision insists on finding its own form and thoroughly usurps the Salinger craftsmanship apparent in earlier work.

The vision to which I have been referring should be perhaps more carefully defined before any detailed examination of *The Catcher in the Rye* and "Seymour: An Introduction." The emergent vision in the whole of Salinger's work is one of the potential of the spiritual self, and the elusiveness of that self, which is always ahead of the movement of the particular moment. He sees the inner self as potentially loving, compassionate, in touch with a human goodness that encompasses the mysteries of the world: in this sense, it is a vision of hope and carries with it a celebration of life. However, the full realization of the compassionate inner self is forever out of reach, because, as is seen in "Seymour," the existential facts of life make the inner self one of the ineluctable mysteries. "Seymour" shows the self as unavailable, no matter how seriously sought, in metaphysical terms expressive of the vision at its fullest. *Catcher* shows the self as unavailable in social terms: the corruption and phoniness of society defeat the strivings for personal and spiritual freedom. But the visionary idea in *Catcher* is betrayed as much by the formal craft of storytelling and its rules, to which Salinger became addicted in his earliest work, as Holden is betrayed by society's insistence that he conform to its rules. But Salinger asks for the safety of conformity (as Holden does not) when he writes *The Catcher in the Rye*: perhaps Salinger's inability to risk his vision here may be understood if the vision is seen as an edge-of-madness one which ultimately involves the writer as much as his subject—a curious phenomenon demonstrated in "Seymour," a story in which Buddy Glass, the writer-narrator of the story, becomes temporarily a madman while trying to capture the essence of a ghost's existential madness.

In *The Catcher in the Rye*, Salinger gives us an open, innocent, protean hero who lives, antisocially, on the periphery of conventional sanity—a modern rebel and existential hero, in fact. And he places this hero in a closed, corrupt, highly structured society, the alleys and byways of which become the ground of his exploration during his journey of adventure, his dark night of the soul during which he wanders through New York City. We would wish to find out, through the representation of this adventure, what can be existentially discovered in such a situation. It would seem that Salinger, along with other contemporary American novelists, such as Malamud in *A New Life* and Bellow in *Henderson the Rain King*, would somehow wish to show the subjective truths of the particularized but protean hero in an open-ended situation. But the overzealous craftsman in Salinger closes the situation: he makes a structure of Holden's "open" character and puts it against the structure of society, thereby intrinsically denying Holden's inner character, his self, at the same time as he sets it in motion in its primal openness, innocence, and claim to authentic discovery. The closed, literary, prestructured character of Holden is embodied in the archetypal figure of Christ, the incongruously ironic hero who, according to Northrop Frye, appears increasingly innocent the more he is punished by society. He is the innocent victim. The archetypal pattern would not of itself suffice to make Holden a closed, labeled hero; it is the enunciating of this pattern in the details of the story that too tightly restricts the movements of the hero. The significance of Holden's dark wandering, full of temptations encountered; the Christmas season setting; Holden's clearly symbolic wish to be the catcher in the rye (that is, the pastoral Jesus figure, a shepherd in the rye field who would save the innocence and purity of the small children, who make up the Salinger "flock," from the fall, the cliff, the dangers beyond the field). These things overwhelm Holden's becomingness with too rigid a pattern of being, and the being is essentially labeled Jesus. If the suffering in Holden's becomingness merely pointed to an archetypal pattern of the incongruously ironic figure, Holden's particularity would not be restricted by the literary device; but in Salinger's structuring, the archetype rules, and we are given a formula for ideal being rather than an urgent existence. We know the end, and in knowing it, we lose the process.

Holden's definition of ideal being is made in response to Phoebe's demand that he name something he would like to be. " 'Like a scientist. Or a lawyer or something.' " It is at this time that Holden verbalizes his choice, a choice against society, and describes his dream of ideality—his wish to be the catcher in the rye—which he will finally achieve in that concluding moment of the narrative action, when he sees that staying with Phoebe is the meaningful gesture he can make, the gesture which "saves" Phoebe, and, fulfilling the Jesus-pattern, puts him into society's hands to be "crucified." The artistry of this; the sense of wholeness achieved in what appears on the surface to be random observations of an adolescent boy; the final paradox—these things evoke in us an admiration for Salinger's craftsmanship and, more than that, for his ability to create a novel, totally modern in its questions, within the context of older novelistic conventions.

But it is just exactly those modern questions which cannot be answered when they are enclosed in the traditions, novelistic or religious, of the past. Holden's questioning of his society makes an insistent claim to fresh insight; it promises more: it promises to shape, through the process of the hero's adventure, something new, if only a new formulation of the question. It is this claim to modern insight which is forfeited when Salinger fails to take the risks his material demands and to strive for the new forms which might make the material manifest. In his later work, the Glass family stories, and especially in "Seymour," even though he very apparently uses Zen ideas, which are after all also given ideas, I think Salinger is a truer artist and is beginning to take the risks his material demands. Seymour, for example, is allowed to be a hero in process, not one imprisoned by a special given literary, mythic, or social idea. Seymour uses all ideas available to this experience; they do not use him. In so doing he shapes his fictive world; Salinger allows him to do this. And it is a risky business, as is attested by the almost unanimously adverse comment on this story. If "warring impulses of the soul distend the shape of Salinger's fiction," as Ihab Hassan suggests, the distended shape is honest and no charge of literary phoniness may be leveled at it.

"Seymour," a long short story, a plotless narrative, details the events, occasions, and gestures of a unique sort of activist; for Seymour, though a situational man in the world (one who responds to occasions rather than inventing them), is an activist of the spirit. In secular situations, he invents his spirit, but he does not invent the situation for the sake of his spirit, or spiritual self, as one might say spiritual activist heroes of other novels do. Given a situation, he transcends it: he does not reject it or change it. Thus, the story of Seymour depends less on his acts and more on his gestures and words, which become significant as the true outward clues to his inner activity. He is the poet or the saint, as Buddy Glass, the writer-narrator, tells us. But Buddy does not merely tell this, as Salinger tells us Holden is the catcher in the rye: he tries to show this, to prove it. In the process of trying to prove Seymour's saintliness, Buddy is afflicted by delirium, mania, chills, and fever which indicate the strain of the task of making manifest in worldly terms the spiritual activity of a living man, dead at the time of the storytelling, a ghost in fact. Buddy is haunted and, therefore, like the Ancient Mariner, somehow compelled to tell the tale. (There is a Gothic-horror quality about this. Perhaps when Salinger first thought of writing a series of stories about the Glass family, he thought in terms of a modern Gothic tale of a dead brother's ghost. However, Salinger's vision is here more metaphysical than Gothic, and there is, I think, no significant horror for the reader.)

While Seymour is the story's hero, who must finally be isolated and discussed, Buddy as narrator has almost as primary a function in the tale as Seymour; for this is as much a story of the process of storytelling as it is a capturing of the process of a saint's life in New York City. It is as if when Salinger risks himself in telling Seymour's story fully he must tell his own, through Buddy. (I do not think he is being coy or cute, as some critics have suggested, when he gives to Buddy biographical data that belong to himself. Rather I think he is honestly attempting to meet the demands made on him by his tale.) That he must tell his own story as the writer seems very suitable on this occasion when his craft is broken by his vision and he searches for new forms that may encompass the largeness and strangeness of the vision. The story is governed by a sense of breakthrough and experiment.

If significant function in the narrative is equally shared by narrator and hero, the story becomes an exemplification of the relationship between the writer and his material; since it is a story, one might say it is, patently, the relationship between the writer and his material. That is always true; here, however, this truth is overt and functional rather than a simple fact of all storytelling.

The story is prefaced by two comments on the act of writing, one by Kafka, one by Kierkegaard. The quotation from Kafka, used as an epigraph for "Seymour," is:

> The actors by their presence always convince me, to my horror, that most of what I've written about them until now is false. It is false because I write about them with steadfast love (even now, while I write it down, this, too, becomes false) but varying ability, and this varying ability does not hit off the real actors loudly and correctly, but loses itself dully in this love that never will be satisfied with the ability and therefore thinks it is protecting this ability from exercising itself.

Kafka is saying that the characters of a writer, once created, have a presence, a reality, in the world, which belongs to them, not to the writer, and that the writer respects this and protects it even from his own craft, which is perhaps mechanical and falsifies the truth the characters have assumed by their viable presence. Kafka's sense of his characters, created by his art but belonging, once there, to the reality of existence, is illustrated in his own work in which the spiritual and secular levels are inextricably joined, creating a thick unity that has seduced scholars and critics to try to separate the parts in order to see what might make such a substantial yet curiously elusive wholeness. Perhaps Salinger is so seduced, but rather than write a critical essay, he brings his question to his own storytelling. He has, until "Seymour," postponed the question, although one sees him working with it in the three earlier long stories about the Glass family, "Franny," "Zooey," and "Raise High the Roof Beam, Carpenters," in which he has, some of the time, permitted his vision to overwhelm simple storytelling techniques, thus encouraging the personae of his characters to emerge more convincingly than they have in the early stories and *Catcher*.

The epigraph from Kierkegaard reads:

> It is (to describe it figuratively) as if an author were to make a slip of the pen, and as if this clerical error became conscious of being such. Perhaps this was no error but in a far higher sense was an essential part of the whole exposition. It is, then, as if this clerical error were to revolt against the author, out of hatred, for him, were to forbid him to correct it, and were to say, "No, I will not be erased, I will

not be erased, I will stand as a witness against thee, that thou art a very poor writer."

Again, this is an enunciation of the writer's creation as having a life of its own, once on the page, once there, even if there by error or accident. Again the material of the work defeats the techniques for its control: a presence once created cannot be dispelled.

The fact of Seymour-as-ghost works as well on this level of the story, which depends upon the dialogue between the writer and his material, as it does on the level of the fictive hero's "simple" story, where saintliness, mysticism, and ghostliness interoperate in a diversity of situation. Seymour, whose death Buddy has depicted in "Perfect Day for Bananafish," must be confronted as a Kafkan "actor" or a Kierkegaardian "clerical error" that achieves presence as he is acknowledged by his creator, the writer. On the level of the writer's awareness, Seymour's ghostliness is interchangeable with this sort of artistic presence, and Buddy, the writer, struggles with it in chills and fever, reminiscent of Kierkegaard's *Fear and Trembling*. Curiously, Buddy the writer recognizes the urgent reality of his actor as Kierkegaard would have the reader know the immediacy of the Abraham and Isaac story and of all stories. But Salinger makes visible, or conscious, this "immediacy" in his story through his creation of a double for himself, Buddy Glass.

It is possible to say that in some way Seymour is also Buddy's double; he is after all his brother, his sharer of a youthful bedroom and of ideas. Buddy is a writer of prose and Seymour is a poet. Both strive to catch and hold for a moment the continuum of poetry they sense flowing through all life. Buddy considers Seymour to have been a true poet although he is unable, finally, to say how or why. (Buddy's failure to say how or why Seymour is a true poet seems appropriate: the mystery of Seymour's poetry remains ultimately inexplicable.)

Seymour is to Buddy as Buddy is to Salinger. If there is indeed a series of doubles here, as there seems to be, then the comment on the creative act and on the immediacy of the created actors (the living relationship between writer and fictive character) is very special and complex. The comment is also singularly modern in its insistence on the dynamics of the creative act itself, and on the creative juggling of the *is* and *is-not* of the two realities: the world's and the work's. This is the literary juggling of what might in the past have been called reality and appearance—but in the past the question has been which, indeed, is which. The "Seymour" story does not give us an ironic picture of a reality controverted by a reality. It comes to no ironic conclusions in areas of necessity, worked through probabilities and the final exhaustion of all possibilities. The novelty of this story is that it is an inconclusive presentation of probabilities which remain probabilities and of possibilities, always open: the story is without ironic undertones.

In his total willingness to suspend judgments, conclusions, answers, and finalities, ironic or not, Salinger achieves two things with the story: uncompromised openness and an affirmation of constant flux. He has, furthermore, erased aesthetic boundaries and aesthetic distance (his own and, with that, the reader's); by determining to recreate experience as experience-in-process and at the same time focusing on the difficulty in the task and the unknowability of reality, he has established spontaneity through seeming chaos (rather than making order out of chaos as is the case in most traditional storytelling). The term "seeming chaos" is used not to suggest that the chaos is accidental but to suggest that the seemingness of this quality is intentionally apparent in the work in which it occurs. A surface chaos is intentional, or, more than that, it is a necessary manifestation on the formal level of the story of the conflict between craft and powerful material. Chaos, never in the history of art and literature considered a formal criterion, becomes in much modern American literature a new dynamic form, reflecting the actual conflict between an outworn traditional form and a new content. The new content, the powerful material, is that of the spirit of man, loosed from its conventional motivations and social modes in literature, art, and religious institutions, but still present to be contended with, accounted for, encountered. If in new literature, madness seems to be the clearer cause for disorder than is spiritual longing, this may be seen as a proof of the struggle with spiritual material that the writer or the hero of the narrative (in the case of "Seymour" both, or all three, if we count the very important Buddy) gives himself to irrationally while half-knowing as he begins that the answers he seeks are by their very nature inaccessible: it is the spiritual adventure that exists in reality which engrosses him; there is no easy conclusion, goal, or answer. The writer knows this and his hero knows this. The task is precipitous since madness is the risk. This risk is clearly indicated in the chaos of such experimental literary work where the destruction of aesthetic limitations, definitions, and aesthetic distance result from the implicit madness (or the choice to live on the edge-of-madness, as Leslie Fiedler has designated the modern spirit-tracking impulse).

Paradoxically, this sort of literature confirms the older aesthetic idea of art as orderly and sane by presenting the reverse of that idea. Perhaps this is the reason that the new activist novel appears to be an anti-art novel, or an anti-novel. In a simpler sense the new novel may be called anti-art because it tries to come closer to life by imitating its literal surface and also by asking metaphysical questions about what is below the surface. Literal reality and serious philosophical questions, combined with the breaking down of aesthetic distance, it may be argued, however, are peculiarly novelistic since the novel has always been extra-literary; it has functioned since the eighteenth century in England as a place for direct commentary on life. When it has not been a commentary on life, it has been a comment on manners. However, the eighteenth- or nineteenth-century novel contained this commentary within clear aesthetic limits or literary conventions. The comment in the new American novel is often referential, unconventional, and uncontained, hence overwhelming, in the work, to the point that the novel often is philosophical more than novelistic in its first commitment, and sometimes prophetic in its final tone.

To weigh an older form against the new, and to call the old "art" and the new "anti-art" is perhaps a merely confusing and misleading comparison, and surely it is an inappropriate stringency. Anti-art is a new form of art; the anti-novel is a new form of novel. It is only necessary to take note of the anti-art (or, here specifically, the anti-novel) idea as such in order to discuss new formalities in the apparent chaos, or "formal discontinuity as a perceptual mode," as one critic recently put it. And it is an interesting fact that the most energetic mainstream in art continues by feeding on all that which traditional art formerly denied. There is inherent in this the demand for reevaluation on all levels.

The "formal discontinuity" of Salinger's story "Seymour" is such a reevaluation. Its distended form is part of that reevaluation, as is the substance of the story dealing with the narrator's conflict with his material. Because Salinger is very aware of what he does here, this story becomes important to the conscious examination of story and novel forms in a way that William Burroughs' fragmentized novel *Naked Lunch* does not. *Naked Lunch*, however, participates just as much in a new formal use of chaos as a constant element as "Seymour" does. It may be more important than "Seymour" because it antedates that story, and in its naturally sprawling, totally undisciplined, drug-addicted way it exists as the ultimate in anti-novel chaos. Yet it is a novel; it is a novel in which the vision of the writer has "destructively" usurped his craft. But the vision is real and powerful; it is so powerful that the serious reader cannot read for any length of time in the book without becoming terrified by the imagery. This, I think, is the reason the book is unreadable. The reason is not the one often given, that is, that the fragmentary pieces of the novel are incoherent to the point of meaninglessness. Incoherent the novel often is, but through this incoherence comes the terrible vision of man's helplessness (man as the naked lunch at the end of the fork) so vivid as to be unreadable, certainly unreadable in any concentrated period of reading time. Burroughs starts where Conrad's "Heart of Darkness" ends—with the horror. He stays always inside the horror, never at a distance from it. And unlike the suggested Gothic horror of "Seymour," the horror of *Naked Lunch* is felt.

Since, unintentionally or intentionally, Burroughs and Salinger dispose of formal distance and the consequent literary structures for their material in *Naked Lunch* and "Seymour," they make language *qua* language do most of the work in their narratives. One is almost tempted to say that it is all done with language. As if language by itself were the last, as it was the first, instrument of the writer. The vision is the language and the form is the language: there is in these writers a linear, fluid verbal surface, a slangy, inventive, witty argot with its own vitality. Burroughs' nonsense lines are as much a part of this rich verbalism as his sensible lines. Sense and nonsense work together. (Having invented a word, Burroughs will give in parentheses, in a solemn dictionarylike way, its definition. For example, when listing the activities of "adolescent hoodlums . . . of all nations" he says they "throw . . . candiru into swimming pools," and in parentheses he defines the candiru, which is a product of his imagination: "the candiru is a small eel-like fish or worm about one-quarter inch through and two inches long patronizing certain rivers of ill-repute in the Greater Amazon Basin.") Burroughs' words add up; they multiply themselves: they become an inundation, a flow that covers the surface, washing away rational conjectures.

Salinger is not so entirely lost inside his vision or its language as Burroughs is; one must, after all, acknowledge that *Naked Lunch* was largely written when Burroughs was in a drug-addicted state and, therefore, immersed in his private vision and its own language. But that fluid, all-pervasive verbalism, so often noticed in Holden's speech in *The Catcher in the Rye*, expands in "Seymour." Buddy talks and talks: the story is a talkathon. Jokes, witticisms, slang, colloquialisms, aphorisms—the stream of language is torrential. Buddy talks compulsively to the reader as if he might lose the ghost of his hero entirely if he permitted a moment of silence. Through the crack of silence, nothingness might enter.

It has been suggested that the verbal flood in "Seymour" is the ultimate exploration of civilized sound, which marks an attempt to exhaust that sound and come finally to a Zen silence. This judgment seems strained to me because, while Salinger is committed to a Zen idea for the saintly character of Seymour, he does not seem to be so committed for himself as a writer. A modern novelist like Jack Kerouac suggests a Zen ideal for the writer himself when he indulges in automatic writing for its own sake in a way that even Burroughs does not. Certainly Salinger nowhere implies that automatic writing is his aim. Buddy, who is a writer, feels cursed by his inability to cope with his saintly brother as hero. Any seeming automatism in the writing of Buddy, and implicitly of Salinger, is not purposeful but rather imposed by the material. The compulsive and automatic talking of Buddy is artfully viewed as a disease, the artist's disease, a "seizure." Art—albeit a new art—is Salinger's undeniable aim, not Zen silence.

Buddy's confrontation with the ghost of his saintly brother has two significant themes: Buddy's theme, the writer and his material, deals with the process of storytelling; the other, Seymour's theme, the saint in the material world, explores the process of saintly and "poetic" living. ("Poetic" adds a new dimension which will be taken up later. I might mention here, however, that Seymour-as-poet is more overtly discussed by Buddy than Seymour-as-saint, though poet and saint overlap; their activities would seem to be, in "Seymour," synonymous. The emphasis on Seymour-as-poet in the secondary theme, Seymour's, complements the primary theme, Buddy's.)

I have already investigated the theme of the writer and his material. To look at the story as it exists on its simplest level, the level which embodies Seymour's theme, one must look at the character created as its hero and at the all-but-plotless plot. Who is Seymour? How does he act? What does he do? Is there a semblance of plot through which the character of the hero is revealed in a series of coherently, causally related moves or acts? There would appear to be no true plot in this essayish confession of a writer; however, there are a group of episodes, seemingly disconnected, which exist in a significant relationship to one another under the surface of the work. These are Seymour's episodes; Seymour is the hero after all, and we are in fact introduced to him as it is Salinger's avowed intention in the title of the piece that we be.

The events or episodes which make up the plot are hidden in among Buddy's digressive comments on writing and his descriptions of Seymour. The references to Seymour first emerge subtly (as later the episodes, told in anecdotal form, will come in quietly and unobtrusively) during the course of Buddy's discussion of the Kierkegaard and Kafka quotations which introduce the story. Kierkegaard and Kafka are two of Buddy's four favorite Sick Men and Great Artists. The other two are Van Gogh and Seymour. Thus Seymour gets on the page; then, in quick succession, this hero goes from Sick Man, to Seer, to Muktah (or Mystic), to Saint, to God-seeker, to Fool, to Poet. All these titles or roles given to Seymour are worked into the fabric of Buddy's discourse on writing, the first section of the total work. In the second section of the work, Buddy discusses the poet and his poetry; the poet is Seymour. There are four anecdotes told. These deal with Seymour as a boy of eight, when he brought the right coat for each guest in his parents' living room to the person to whom it belonged without having foreknowledge of the ownership of the coat; as a boy of eleven, when he first discovered poetry books in the library; as a boy of fourteen, when he constantly jotted down poems wherever he was; as an older boy, when he tried to find a poetry form for his "un-Western" vision. There is also mention of his suicide, after which was found one of four poems paraphrased by Buddy. This second section, focusing on the poet and his poetry, ends with a depiction of the literary scene in America, complete with Buddy's amusing concession that critics are not fools because Seymour had said that Christ meant that there were no fools when He said "call no man Fool." In connection with literary gossip,

Buddy paraphrases the fourth Seymour poem about a wise old man who, dying, would rather eavesdrop on gossiping in the courtyard than listen to the learned talk in his room.

In the first section we have met Seymour and learned of his several "heroic" roles; in the second section, we have seen him as mystic and poet, heard him talk as saint and poet. In the third section, we have the history of the family which has produced this hero. The family ancestry includes a juggling Polish Jewish clown, an Irish tramp, and Les and Bess, the father and mother who were vaudeville stars. Seymour as poet becomes Seymour as juggler of experience: deep personal experience is balanced with autobiographical experience in his haiku-like poems—that is, while the poems are intensely personal, they are not factually autobiographical: a remarkable feat which Buddy finds a juggling feat.

The fourth section returns to literature, with the emphasis directly on Buddy's writing rather than on Seymour's poetry; however, Seymour is now very much in the piece, and it is on his comments about Buddy's stories that the fourth section concentrates. This section is a new start in a way: at the very beginning of the story we have had Buddy's comments on writing and writers, leading to Seymour's appraisal of him as prose writer. An intricate twist, this return is properly introduced by Buddy's declaration that he has been away from the story and the reader, suffering from acute hepatitis, for nine weeks. He takes us back to the beginning, when he announced his manic happiness to have been an artist's seizure, a compulsion to speak. Perhaps, he says now, he was only liverish; what brings him from his literal sickness now to re-encounter Seymour is an old note of Seymour's, dealing with a 1940 story of Buddy's. The story goes from this note to others until the sum of Seymour's critical thoughts on writing is finally revealed: writing is a religious activity. It is necessary, therefore, to write one's heart out. Writing the heart out is more important, more germinal to the writer, than writing a masterpiece. " 'I want your *loot*,' " not some neat formulized tricks, Seymour tells the young story writer, Buddy. " 'Trust your heart,' " he adds. By way of bolstering these critical insights and dicta of Seymour to Buddy, there are more episodes, anecdotally told, involving Seymour and Buddy as adults. Without the reader's noticing, Seymour has grown up. There are, in the fourth section, fewer tales of his childhood, more tales of his mature activity and thought. However, childlikeness pervades his personality. Adulthood does not change the nature of his innocence.

The last and most important section of the story might be called Seymour as corporeal being. Since this story is about Seymour, who was almost all spirit in life, and is literally all spirit at the time of writing, this fifth and last section, which takes more than one-third of the story's 137 pages, is an attempt on Buddy's part to keep Seymour on the page, to give him material being, in "life" and in literature, the dual task of Buddy the brother and Buddy the writer. As Buddy goes through the specifics of describing Seymour's earthly appearance, there is a paradoxical intensifying of Seymour's otherworldliness. The random list, a device of many contemporary American novelists, makes its appearance in this section as an element of structure. Nose, wrists, hair, hands, teeth—all of these fall into line, but without apparent order. One physical aspect grows out of a story about another. The organization is linear, not gestalt, and Buddy makes a special point of repudiating cubist theories of art that might be applied to his attempt to see the parts of Seymour at the same time that he sees the whole of Seymour, to see a point in time in Seymour's life at the same time that he sees all of Seymour's life. Buddy says, always keeping his focus on Seymour and Seymour's thoughts, even while discussing his own ideas of prose writing:

> It wouldn't worry [Seymour] a very great deal, I think, if after due consultation with my instincts I elected to use some sort of literary Cubism to present his face. For that matter, it wouldn't worry him at all if I wrote the rest of this exclusively in lower-case letters—if my instincts advised it. I wouldn't *mind* some form of Cubism here, but every last one of my instincts tells me to put up a good, lower-middle-class fight against it.

Buddy, as usual, puts down the literary label, whether Freudian or cubist or other, before it comes up. He is being, above all else, honest, as Seymour would have him be. (Alfred Chester notes *Salinger*'s honesty in writing this story; he calls it "courageous" and suggests its honesty be compared to the dishonesty of earlier Salinger stories. Salinger, through Buddy, keeps his effort at honesty in the foreground.)

Sticking to his linear organization of this final section, Salinger allows Buddy to leap from physical feature to physical feature until he lands in the description of the essence of Seymour's physicality—Seymour's inexplicable athletic prowess—based on a formlessness which for anyone but Seymour would have led to a loss of control in games such as tennis, Ping-Pong, stoopball, pocket pool, and curb marbles. The curb marbles anecdote, set in a time-suspended moment on a New York City sidewalk, is the appropriate climax of the whole story; it is not a climax in the usual sense of the culmination and coming together of several strands of action in a story but rather in the sense of the high moment (perhaps to be compared to Joyce's epiphany, although epiphany, as Joyce defines and exploits it, is even more a mysteriously poetic, organic, and final revelatory moment) when the reader feels that he at last has "the loot"—Salinger's loot, Buddy's loot, and Seymour's loot: the metaphysical loot of the story which goes beyond the story. And the reader gets to his point not with a sense of consummation and conclusion but with a sense of a meaningful respite in a continuum that extends outside the story and past its final sentences.

The curb marbles episode is, again, anecdotal and tells of a ten-year-old Seymour, a figure coming into the field of marble-playing through the shadows of a city dusk ("his face shadowed, dimmed out"—that physical face which Buddy has just gone to great trouble to capture, pin down on the page, piece by piece, returns for this scene to immateriality); he sees the game that Buddy, a boy of eight, is playing with a friend, and advises Buddy on his playing. Two things Seymour says at this time stand out particularly: " 'Could you try not aiming so much?' " and " 'If you hit him when you aim, it'll just be luck.' " Seymour walks toward the two marble players; and Buddy quickly breaks up the game. Several pages later, just before the last pages of the story, Buddy interprets Seymour's advice:

> When he was coaching me, from the curbstone across the street, to quit aiming my marble at Ira Yankauer's—and he was ten, please remember—I believe he was instinctively getting at something very close in spirit to the sort of instructions a master archer in Japan will give when he forbids a willful new student to aim his arrows at the target; that is, when the archery master permits, as it were, Aiming but no aiming.

Buddy goes on from here to disclaim the wish to make a one-to-one relationship between Seymour's instruction and Zen instruction. He insists that he himself is Zenless though interested in the classical Zen writings; that Zen is in disrepute because it has been dirtied by popularizers who make of Zen detachment "an invitation to spiritual disinterestedness"; that pure Zen will survive however. But the comparison between Seymour and the Zen archery teacher stands, and Seymour's Zenfulness, as opposed to Buddy's Zenlessness, stands. The heart of the curb marbles anecdote is the sense of formlessness as value; deliberate formal aiming corrupts because it betokens a belief that one may or may not hit his target. Formlessness assumes that one naturally, intuitively, instinctively hits the target. The arrow is made for the bull's-eye, the thrown marble for the stationary marble. The man attuned to the game, the true player, stands between the two—arrow and bull's-eye, marble and marble. He can best be an intermediary by shunning formal, external, given rules or forms for the game, by simply playing.

In life, as in games, the Seymour-hero goes, without method, rule, or external form, from "one little piece of Holy Ground to the next." In life, which is a meta-game, formlessness is still the rule (or nonrule). (In spite of Buddy's insistence on his own Zenlessness, he has adopted Seymour's nonrule formlessness for this story, the implication being that he must since Seymour is its hero and the story shapes itself in acquiescence to the hero and his gestures and acts.) It is because Seymour makes of life a meta-game that excludes worldly social and ethical rules of conduct and depends instead upon a formlessness in responses which are dictated by an awareness and "feel" for any particular situation that I call him a spiritual hero.

Since Salinger, through the narration of Buddy, explores possible formula types, or archetypes, for Seymour (Sick Man, Poet, Mystic, Saint) and is forced always beyond each of these by the nature of his hero, he is finally committed to a description of Seymour's existential being, unformulated and loose, as it confronts the thick and secular world. The question posed (more posed than answered) by Seymour's behavior is the question of what is spirit in the modern world, on the street, released from religious institutions? How does the spirit function, act, and move? Seymour's existential being is to be understood as a cipher for spirituality. (The initial S. is sometimes used by Buddy to stand for Seymour and seems more of an indication of the nature of the hero as cipher than it does a mere abbreviation of the name.) Buddy's strenuous effort to capture the material substance of his brother Seymour is an inverse way of showing us that this is impossible and of proving Seymour's existence to have been almost wholly a matter of spirituality, not physicality. Seymour does not live in a secular world but redefines the world of things in his own terms so that he goes from one piece of holy ground to the next. It is not necessary for him to rebel against the secular as it is found in the community (the village in *The Castle*), for he does not recognize the community. He sees only individuals and he sees only one group, the family group. The family is so thoroughly released from everyday concerns (in spite of the Glass parents' concern when Waker gives away his new Davega bicycle) and its members are so much more spiritual descendants of clowns and hoboes than they are New Yorkers that Seymour's willing and intimate involvement with them puts no strain on his secularly ignorant spirituality.

As has been said, Seymour makes of life a spiritual metagame, in which the only code is formlessness. The object of the game seems to be that the man be an intermediary between one concreteness and another for the sake of an undefined but absolute spirit. In the guise of poet, for example, Seymour, writing his own brand of double haiku, brings the red balloon, or the old wise man, or the widower to language. He makes himself a passive connection between the thing-in-life and the language. The double haiku, invented by Seymour, represents the loosening of an already "formless" form, the Japanese haiku, which restrains the poem only in number of lines and syllables. The only reason he looks for a form at all is so that he may write poems that will be understood by his favorite librarian. He does need a form in order to communicate, but he finds only a tenuous one, as a gesture of love. In the passive, innocent, mediating role that Seymour plays as a primary stance in his life meta-game (the corollary roles to this total one are those of mystic, poet, teacher, et cetera), love is not a commitment but a natural, effortless gesture. Seymour overcomes alienation and nothingness, those twin curses of modern life, by turning alienation into the necessary solitary independence of the saintly and spiritual man and by turning nothingness into a formlessness to be celebrated. The modern traumas are grist for his particular mill.

"To unlearn the illusory differences: this is what for Salinger it means *to be as a child*. And the Glasses, we remember, are in this sense children, holy innocents still at twenty or thirty or forty." If Seymour is in the serene state of being of a child, free of the illusory differences of worldliness, he is in a state of lyrical freedom which K. partially achieves in what Paul Goodman calls "manic responses in abnormal states of consciousness" and finds in four particular lyrical passages in *The Castle*: the walk through the snowy night with Barnabas; the encounter with Frieda under the bar; the wait for Klamm in the snow; the bedroom scene with the castle official, Bürgel. Goodman also speaks of the "turmoil of conflicting plots" in *The Castle*: "[The conflicting plots] are in two sets: K.'s purpose and the high authorities; and the village, Frieda . . . —and this turmoil is so managed and so kept in motion by the protagonist's character . . . that it can never come to an end." But, he says, the lyrical passages interrupt the turmoil and hold the possibility of a resolution. The protagonist is "watchful, willful, and stubborn," and Goodman contends that the "pattern of the book . . . is to exhaust him and carry him away with the satisfaction that comes with finally giving in." He adds: "We must envisage a resolution passage in the ending not unlike the four just quoted, but with one important difference: it is not manic. . . . it is an open-eyed view of the actual scene and *therefore* spontaneous and unwilled." This finding from an analysis of the structure of *The Castle* is very ingenious, but I do not think the abnormal lyric passages necessarily point to a consummation in the grace of a lyrical resolution. Grace, through access to the castle, may be that toward which K. strives, but his existence as hero depends upon the process of striving; he is watchful and willful, aware and active. That his story ends without resolution, without a true conclusion, seems appropriate to the full realization of his character, his existence. Seymour, on the other hand, is constantly in this state of formless lyrical freedom and grace and not abnormally or manically so. He is never so because he is drunk, sleepy, or involved in sexual fantasy, as is K. in the lyrical passages Goodman cites. The striving for the castle is Buddy's. Buddy becomes the Kafkan hero, and Seymour is his castle. Shall we ask ourselves of Seymour, as we do of the castle, is he diabolic or divine? And does it matter? To the story *qua* story I think it does not matter.

The definition of spirit lies as much in the process of attempting its capture in language as it does in the description of Seymour which finally evolves, and the twofold structure of the "Seymour" story rests on the process of description as well as on the ultimate description.

Spirit may be diabolic or divine in the modern world. It is sought for itself. It would seem not to matter very much in which direction the spiritual activist goes in the modern world, up, down, sideways, in circles, so long as he goes, *moves*. Erich Heller, after discussing the modern loss of "the relation between mundane and transcendental reality," with the transcendental, or spiritual, losing its validity in a positivistic-scientific time and the mundane "becoming more 'really' real than before," says that by Kafka's time "reality has been all but completely sealed off against any transcendental intrusion" and that, therefore, in Kafka's world the "heroes struggle in vain for spiritual survival." He continues, "Thus [Kafka's] creations are symbolic, for they are infused with . . . negative transcendence." It is because K. does *not* gain the castle (or finally give in to the lyrical state of consciousness which Goodman speaks of) and because Buddy remains Zenless and cannot firmly capture the essential nature of Seymour's existence that K. and Buddy both seem to be literary heroes created in the terms of the most honest modernist vision of the spiritual quest, and its inevitable failure.

BERNICE GOLDSTEIN AND
SANFORD GOLDSTEIN

Zen and Nine Stories

Why did Salinger affix to *Nine Stories* the Zen *koan* which questions the disciple about the sound of one hand clapping? Since Salinger had seriously started his study of Zen after World War II and since he has continued it with increasing interest up through the writing of "Hapworth 16, 1924," his latest story, the hand-clapping koan was not merely arbitrary, especially when one considers that eight of the stories in the collection had appeared earlier in magazines.

Zen overtones are perhaps strongest in "Teddy." When Nicholson, the teacher of education, asks Teddy what he would do if he could change the educational system in our country, the boy replies:

> "I know I'm pretty sure I wouldn't start with the things schools usually start with . . . . I think I'd first just assemble all the children together and show them how to meditate. I'd try to show them how to find out who they *are*, not just what their names are and things like that . . . I guess, even before that, I'd get them to empty out everything their parents and everybody ever told them. I mean even if their parents just told them an elephant's big, I'd make them empty *that* out. An elephant's only big when it's next to something else—a dog or a lady, for example . . . . I wouldn't even tell them an elephant has a trunk. I might *show* them an elephant, if I had one handy, but I'd let them just walk up to the elephant not knowing anything more about it than the elephant knew about *them*. The

From *Renascence: Essays on Values in Literature* 22, no. 4 (Summer 1970). © 1970 by the Catholic Renascence Society, Inc.

same thing with grass, and other things. I wouldn't even tell them
grass is green . . . . It makes them start expecting the grass to look a
certain way—*your way*—instead of some other way that may be
just as good, and maybe much better . . . I don't know. I'd just make
them vomit up every bit of the apple their parents and everybody
made them take a bite out of."

Teddy's last sentence in the above quotation, a most suggestive one, thrusts the
reader into the very effect that the koan struggle leads to. To vomit up every bit
of the apple, to struggle with the paradoxical so that the mind itself is at the very
last edge of the abyss where reason can no longer divide, separate, categorize—
such ought to be the positive effect of the koan.

On the other hand, the koan exercise, says Heinrich Dumoulin in his *History of Zen Buddhism*, can lead to disaster: "The unnatural suppression of
reason is a gamble. It may destroy the psychic structure of a person permanently
and irremediably. The inviolable dignity of man sets limits to the koan exercise
as well as to the therapeutic process of modern psychiatry."

It seems to us that one approach to *Nine Stories* is through an examination
of these two extremes of the koan experience. In one instance the struggle with a
particular insoluble problem that is beyond the realm of the rational may lead
to mental breakdown; in the other, the struggle with a problem beyond the
guidelines of reason may lead to enlightenment, satori. That *Nine Stories* ends
with two narratives whose characters reach a satori of one kind or another
indicates the positive force Salinger's stories have taken.

The originator of the "sound-of-one-hand" koan was Hakuin (1685–
1768), called the greatest of the Japanese Zen masters. When he was an old
man, Dumoulin notes, he devised this koan as "a problem which he believed
would penetrate into one's consciousness with incomparable sharpness and would
readily lead to the awakening of doubt and to progress in the exercises." Dumoulin translates Hakuin's koan: "If someone claps his hands, one hears a sound at
once. Listen now to the sound of a single hand!" What the "solution" to the
koan means continues Dumoulin is that "He who lifts one hand and while
listening quietly can hear a sound which no ears hear, can surpass all conscious
knowledge. He can leave the world of distinctions behind him; he may cross the
ocean of the *karma* of rebirths, and he may break through the darkness of
ignorance. In the enlightenment he attains to unlimited freedom."

This unlimited freedom, at least in the Western meaning of the phrase,
seems best reached by children. In those children whose imaginative machinery
has not yet been broken by demanding parents, in those children who do not yet
rationalize every action, whose transitions jerk joyfully from one point to another

without self-consciousness or even with revenge or demonic joy, in those children whose spontaneity comes as easily as breath and whose minds have not yet dichotomized language, persons, places, things—to these children belong that state of enlightenment which the struggle with koan leads to.

The example in *Nine Stories* which readily comes to mind is "Uncle Wiggily in Connecticut." The child Ramona with her childlike spontaneous imaginative power is on the verge of having these qualities eradicated by her mother, ironically referred to as "Uncle Wiggily." It is Ramona who scratches when she feels like scratching, who picks her nose when the nose demands picking, and who can easily murder her latest "invisible" companion, Jimmy Jimmereeno. Yet, it is Ramona who wears glasses, a Ramona whose vision of some other world is so concrete that even as she sleeps, she leaves room in bed for her "imaginary" playmate, a playmate so "real" that it walks with her, has a sword, and is without freckles. Eloise's symbolic gesture at the end of the story, a gesture that finds her replacing her daughter's glasses lens down—the child herself had set them down carefully, "folded neatly and laid stems down"—reveals the lack of vision of the adult whose perpetual conflict is her marriage to her husband and the death of the spontaneous Walt. Eloise vividly recalls an occasion when, on the train from Trenton to New York, Walt had placed his hand on her stomach. This Zen-like irrational gesture after a moment of insight is indicated when Eloise says: " 'All of a sudden he said my stomach was so beautiful he wished some officer would come up and order him to stick his other hand through the window. He said he wanted to do what was fair. Then he took his hand away and told the conductor to throw his shoulders back. He told him if there was one thing he couldn't stand it was a man who didn't look proud of his uniform.' "

The puzzle to Western readers may arise when Eloise says Walt " 'wanted to do what was fair.' " Being fair from a Zen point of view is not to separate joy from pain; it means that "beauty" or "pain" or "death" or "sorrow" is not a separate category in which things, moments, persons are given names, are described by adjectives. Walt is well on the road to awareness. The state of being a *general* in the army does not, to Walt's way of thinking, indicate five stars but nakedness with a small infantry button stuck in the navel. That is to say, to be at the "heights" from the Zen point of view is to reduce the self to its barest quality of identity with all things, all beings. The navel suggests the position in meditation where the discursive intellect can no longer intrude.

Like Franny, Zooey, and Buddy before the stage of partial enlightenment, Eloise, as her friend Mary Jane indicates, is far too critical. Eloise criticizes Ramona for her boots, scratching, nose-picking; the maid for not knowing where things are or how to clean; her husband for his lack of intelligence, his petty jealousies, his admiration for the writings of L. Manning Vines. When her husband telephones to ask about a ride home and when the maid Grace asks if her own husband can spend the night, Eloise rudely rejects both requests. After going up to see Ramona, Eloise jars the child into wakefulness and complains about the space left in bed for Ramona's new playmate Mickey Mickeranno. Once more downstairs, Eloise staggers in her drunken condition, the noise waking Mary Jane. In a kind of chant of despair, Eloise raises the unanswerable question: " 'I was a nice girl . . . wasn't I?' " We discover Eloise is unable to solve the puzzle of her existence, the why of what she is, what she has become, the childish "Uncle Wiggily" quality dormant within her. We feel that Eloise, like so many of Salinger's psychologically disturbed characters, is almost on the verge of a nervous breakdown.

A further instance of the destruction of the spontaneous, irrational, and imaginative world of a child occurs in "The Laughing Man." The narrator looks back to a traumatic moment in his childhood when he belonged to the Comanche Club, whose Chief is interestingly enough a twenty-two or -three-year-old student of *law* at N.Y.U., a man the narrator describes as extremely shy and gentle, yet an "almost-All-American tackle of 1926," and a good enough baseball player who had once been invited to try out for the New York Giants. The everlasting adventures of the Laughing Man, the hero of a series of fantastic episodes, have such an effect on the nine-year-old that "You could always take it home with you and reflect on it while sitting, say, in the out-going water in the bathroom." The Laughing Man's face has been so hideously disfigured by bandits that he covers it with a "pale" red gossamer mask made out of poppy petals. It is the cruel stripping away of the mask in the last episode the Chief tells that provides the key symbol of the story, for the Chief, finally confronted with the reality of his own situation in life, destroys the Laughing Man and in effect the Club itself. When the Chief learns he has made Mary Hudson pregnant (the conflict is alluded to when the narrator feels Mary Hudson had dropped out of the lineup permanently: "It was the kind of whole certainty, however independent of the sum of its facts, that can make walking backwards more than normally hazardous, and I bumped smack into a baby carriage") and after Mary Hudson runs off the baseball field crying, the Chief returns dejectedly to the bus and angrily begins his continuation of the episode begun earlier the same day. What jolts his youthful listeners is the slow death of the Laughing Man, who, bleeding, face uncovered, appeals to the forest animals for help. The lovable dwarf Omba is summoned by the animals, but by the time he arrives, the Laughing Man is in a coma. The very last act of mercy is for Omba to retrieve his master's mask. When the Laughing Man opens his eyes and calls for his beloved timberwolf, Black Wing, only to learn of the animal's death, he crushes the life-saving vial of eagle's blood and, ordering Omba to turn away, pulls off his own mask and dies. One of the young listeners bursts into tears, and the then-nine-year-old narrator, after leaving the bus, happens to see "a piece of red tissue paper flapping in the wind against the base of a lamppost. It looked like someone's poppy-petal mask."

In non-Zen terms the rational adult world confronted by an impossible choice reacts in a logically rational way. Mary Hudson cannot allow herself to remain pregnant without demanding marriage; the Chief cannot afford to marry and interrupt his law degree; the irrational, spontaneous fantasy world of the Laughing Man cannot be permitted to continue; and the children themselves must be cruelly stripped of the truly "real" world, the poppy-mask of the Laughing Man so real that the nine-year-old arrives home "teeth chattering uncontrollably" after his view of the piece of red tissue against the lamppost. That the story is one of a negative initiation into the restricting qualities of the unenlightened adult world is indicated by the narrator's comment early in the story:

> In 1928 . . . I regarded myself not only as the Laughing Man's direct descendant but as his only legitimate living one. I was not even my parents' son in 1928 but a devilishly smooth imposter, awaiting their slightest blunder as an excuse to move in—preferably without violence, but not necessarily—to assert my true identity. As a precaution against breaking my bogus mother's heart, I planned to take her into my underworld employ in some undefined but appropriately regal capacity. But the *main* thing I had to do in 1928 was watch my step. Play along with the force. Brush my teeth. Comb my hair. At all costs, stifle my natural hideous laughter.

The Chief, like Eloise, is at that stage in life where he too questions the meaning of his existence, and, like Eloise, who puts the glasses lens down and distorts the *real* real, the Chief strips away the mask of laughter, of irrational exuberance, of the transitional jerk where one can cross the border from China into France, where in effect one can hear the sound of a single hand.

"Uncle Wiggily in Connecticut" and "The Laughing Man" are stories in which seemingly insoluble problems in the adult world mar the Zen-like world of children. The same kind of situation can be demonstrated in "Down at the Dinghy." But what about the world of children which affects the adult world in some radically significant way? We wish to consider from this focus "A Perfect Day for Bananafish" and "For Esmé—with Love and Squalor," at the same time keeping in mind the basic impact of koan either to lead one to unrelieved desperation or to free one toward the way, the path toward enlightened perception.

"A Perfect Day for Bananafish" is perhaps the cul-de-sac of all Salinger's efforts during more than twenty years of intense creativity. The easy way out of the problem raised by the stories about Seymour Glass is to indicate that Salinger's conception of Seymour has been undergoing change since the story was first published, that the early story ought to have no relationship to the later stories, and that "A Perfect Day for Bananafish" ought to be treated intrinsically. That the story can be read as an isolated entity is certainly feasible, but the fact remains that the later stories continually refer to Seymour's suicide so that Salinger himself insists on working his way through the dilemma of his own major creative koan. How can one who has heard the sound of a single hand commit suicide? That Seymour has been enlightened is the continual implication in the later stories about him. It seems to us that Seymour's dilemma is that of the enlightened man rejected by the non-enlightened world, the major conflict in "Raise High the Roof Beam, Carpenters" and "Hapworth 16, 1924."

With these considerations in mind we wish to further point out, however, that satori is not a constant. The solution of one koan may lead to enlightenment, but one such moment of this kind, important as it is, is not necessarily the deepest.

The moment of satori may, in fact, be for only a brief interlude. The disciple may feel he has broken through the barriers to the penetration of the "real" only to find himself forced back to greater effort, greater concentration, a deeper probing and penetration. The case of Hakuin is pertinent. Dumoulin quotes Hakuin's description of his first enlightenment:

> "During the spring of my twenty-fourth year I was staying at the Eiganji Temple in the province of Echigo where I practiced assiduously. I slept neither by day nor by night, and forgot both to rest and to eat. Suddenly I was overcome by the Great Doubt. I felt as though freezing in an ice field extending thousands of miles. My bosom was filled with an extraordinary purity. I could neither advance nor retire. It was as if I were out of my mind and only the word 'nothing' remained. During the lecture I heard, indeed, the explanations of the master, but it was as if I heard a discourse from afar in a distant Zen hall. Sometimes I felt as if I were floating through the air. This state continued for a number of days until one night while hearing the striking of the temple bell I experienced the transformation.
>
> "It was like the smashing of a layer of ice, or the pulling down of a crystal tower. As I suddenly awakened and came to my senses . . . [all] former doubts were fully dissolved like ice which melted away. With a loud voice I called out. 'How glorious, how glorious!' We

need no escape from the cycle of life and death, nor need we strive after enlightenment. The seventeen hundred *koan* exercises are not worthy of being posed. My pride rose up like a mountain and my exaltation welled up like a flood. To myself I thought that for two or three hundred years there had been no sudden breakthrough like mine, with such great ecstasy. With this vision I immediately set out on the road to Shinano."

Dumoulin continues:

Convinced that he had attained the enlightened state, Hakuin set out to report the good news to Etan, the aged hermit at Shojuan in the district of Shinano. The master received him, and Hakuin described the experience for his approval and handed over his verses on enlightenment. What followed is one of those unique scenes, full of originality, wit, and crudeness, which have belonged to the Zen tradition. . . . Master Etan took up the verses in his left hand and said, "This you have learned. This is your theoretical knowledge. Now show me your own intuitive insight, your enlightenment," and at the same time he held out his right hand. Without hesitation Hakuin rejected the master's verdict that his enlightenment was inadequate. A sharp argument followed, at the end of which the old monk twisted Hakuin's nose, saying "You poor child of the devil in the dark dungeon!"

Hakuin had to return to practice further.

What is so remarkable about the Seymour Glass of "A Perfect Day for Bananafish" is his understanding of children. What is equally remarkable is Salinger's ability to evoke the non sequitur world of children, their logical illogicality. Seymour is so attuned to the world of Sibyl that he can respond with almost perfect spontaneity to the spontaneous overflow of joy, of seriousness, of destruction even, of Sibyl's own verbal agility. Only when she asks Seymour if he likes wax does he momentarily have to "think" by repeating part of her question. When Sibyl says she likes to chew candles, Seymour replies, " 'Who doesn't?' " When she objects to his statement about the tigers and corrects him by noting there were only six going round the tree, Seymour says, " '*Only* six! . . . Do you call that *only?*' " Seymour responds enthusiastically when Sibyl claims she saw a bananafish, and he immediately asks if there were any bananas in its mouth. When Sibyl answers six, Seymour bows before her superior imaginative, irrational power—he kisses the arch of one of her wet feet. When she objects with " 'Hey!' " Seymour retorts, " 'Hey, yourself!' " They are almost perfectly attuned with no line of separation between the adult world and the world of the child. It is not surprising then that Sibyl is continually on the lookout for Seymour, much to the annoyance of her mother, whose main aim seems to be to gossip and drink martinis.

As we later discover in "The Laughing Man," the story told to a child contains the seeds of a future destruction. In the bananafish story Seymour's dreadful dilemma is revealed. But earlier the drifting allusion to Eliot's *The Waste Land*, "Mixing memory and desire," returns the reader to the opening scene of Muriel's conversation with her mother. That the world outside of Seymour is ruled by dichotomies is suggested in the first paragraph reference to the article Muriel has just finished reading, "Sex is Fun—or Hell." Over the phone Muriel answers her mother's objections to Seymour's having driven during the trip down to Florida by assuring her parent: " 'I asked him to stay close to the white line.' " The title Seymour has supposedly given to his wife is "Spiritual Tramp." Muriel objects to the removal of class distinctions at the hotel as she complains about the couple that sits next to her table for, as she says, their appearance suggests they drove to the hotel in a truck. Above all, however, the uniquely "real" world of Sibyl contrasts painfully with the self-conscious, ego-burdened, phony world of adults. After the experience of Sibyl's devastatingly honest confrontation with the here and now, it is no wonder that Seymour is annoyed at the passive voyeurism of the lady on the elevator. When he enters his hotel room, the smell of new calf-skin luggage and "nail-lacquer *remover*" (italics ours) reminds him once more of the adult world of separation, of show and tell. The room itself takes on the characteristics of a bananafish hole. Seymour is surfeited, unable to find his way out except through suicide. What he has been unable to sustain is the non-phony world of the child. He has, in fact, been trying to keep to the line, the white line of sanity, a metaphorical tightrope in which he must stay away from trees, not expose his tattoo, say the right thing to Granny, see his psychiatrist. Whatever in Seymour's past made him cognizant of the Zen-like world of children has broken down. The reality of the phony-world becomes too great to bear.

"For Esmé—with Love and Squalor," on the other hand, finds Sergeant X surviving the devastating squalor of war through the irrational response of not a Sibyl, but an Esmé, certainly an emerald in the rough in spite of Esmé's attempts to enter the phony class. Yes, Esmé is pompous, conceited, a misuser of words; at the same time she is that spontaneous effervescent adolescent who has come to be part of the myth of innocence, of naiveté, pseudosophistication, youth. She asks the Sergeant to write her a story of squalor, for she's "extremely" interested in the subject, much as a juvenile might say he likes TV or Gary Cooper. What makes Esmé a joy for the reader is her verbal overflow. Later in the story, in her letter of June 7, 1944, the same spontaneity gushes forth. Her precise calculation of the elapse of time since they met (thirty-eight days), the rendering of the time of her interview (between 3:45 and 4:15 P.M. on April 30, 1944), is as childlike as her noting that she had not even observed if the soldier in question had a watch. The incongruity of the situation of sending a watch that can give the "velocity one is walking" at after a D-Day invasion needs no further comment. But an indirect comment of Salinger's does, for when Esmé writes that she hopes D-Day "will bring about the swift termination of the war and a method of existence that is ridiculous to say the least," Salinger seems to be implying that a more irrational view of life, one in which the ridiculous plays a greater role, is essential.

"De Daumier-Smith's Blue Period" is saturated with aspects of the irrational. In fact, the first sentence is pertinent: "If it made any real sense—and it doesn't even begin to." The story, of course, makes very good sense, though readers may at first be puzzled by its seemingly illogical organization. First we are told by the narrator that he has laboriously begrudged his stepfather, Robert Agadganian, Jr., the adjectives "adventurous, magnetic . . . and generous." In fact, Salinger uses the word "picaresque" adjectives, the word picaresque suggesting the supposedly haphazard structure of the story and the comic "roguelike" qualities of the narrator-hero. The first real incident in the story concerns the nineteen-year-old narrator on a New York bus when, after the bus driver profanely tells the young passenger to "move that ass," the narrator, in French, informs the driver that he considers him a "rude, stupid, overbearing imbecile." The next "adventure" occurs when the narrator steps out of the Ritz Hotel. Seeing the chaos on the New York streets, he prays "for the city to be cleared of people, for the gift of being alone—a-l-o-n-e." He loathes the art school he attends. Three late afternoons a week he goes to the dentist (in two months eight of his teeth were pulled, three front ones). On other afternoons the narrator all but "hisses" at the American entries in the art galleries. To annoy his stepfather, he buys a complete set of the *Harvard Classics*, these for evening reading. At night the young man paints, though at times, feeling capricious, he draws cartoons. The situation with his stepfather is politely murderous.

With the foregoing as background, Salinger gets to the key episode (really a string of episodes). Interestingly enough, the name of the school the narrator applies to teach at is called "Les Amis Des Vieux Maîtres," the antagonistic narrator no doubt hung up by the word "amis." The narrator's letter of application is a series of lies. As participant in a world in which bus drivers have no respect for anyone, it hardly seems as if an honest application can even receive a mild letter of rejection. As the narrator goes to post his letter, he asks the Ritz mail clerk ("who unmistakably loathed" him) to keep on the alert for a letter addressed to Daumier-Smith, the pseudonym adopted by the narrator. Later that day he finds his anatomy class members a "fairly decent bunch," this for the first time yet no doubt because he feels he will soon be rid of them. On receiving his letter of appointment to the school, the narrator is told by M. Yoshoto to report June 23 in order to learn about his duties and "to become firm friends" with the other instructors, M. Yoshoto referring to himself as the new employee's "new friend and employer." Later that evening when Daumier-Smith wants to break the news to Bobby, he meets an attractive guest whom Daumier-Smith characterizes as a "charming person whose every attempt to be friendly to me, to gently persuade me to take off my armor—or at least my helmet" he chooses to interpret as an invitation to join in bed.

When Daumier-Smith arrives at Windsor Station in Montreal, about the only thing he has a "high opinion of" (having in every phase of the story thus far rejected all mankind) is his "double-breasted, beige gabardine suit." His meeting with M. Yoshoto does not help to dispel any of this criticism against mankind, and Daumier-Smith is so nonplussed by the silent, inscrutable quality of the school director that previous lies are magnified. Interestingly enough, Daumier-Smith criticizes Picasso for never listening "to anybody—even his closest friends."

The end of Daumier-Smith's "blue period," that is, the end of his despondent view of life, begins with his entrance into Les Amis Des Vieux Maîtres, located symbolically enough over an orthopedic appliance shop. Daumier-Smith is first jolted by a beautifully simple watercolor hanging on the wall in the one large room that is the school itself: "Occasionally, I still dream of a certain white goose flying through an extremely pale-blue sky . . . —the blueness of the sky, or an ethos of the blueness of the sky, reflected on the bird's feathers." With the Yoshoto family, however, the isolation of Daumier-Smith increases. He spends a sleepless night in the absent son's room, hears the strange moans in the sleep of one of the Yoshotos, eats breakfast in silence as M. Yoshoto reads a Japanese newspaper, sits (in a blue suit) at his isolated desk an hour and a half before he is given anything to do, only to be handed the task of translating French notes into English for M. Yoshoto.

Daumier-Smith's comments on M. Yoshoto's corrections are revealing, for they foreshadow the gift that will be Daumier-Smith's to give away. Daumier-Smith says M. Yoshoto's ability is merely to give his students something recognizable, that is to say, he can teach a student how to draw a "recognizable pig in a recognizable sty, or even a picturesque pig in a picturesque sty." But a beautiful pig in a beautiful sty was not part of the director's spiritual equipment—not that Daumier-Smith is disturbed by "this ruthless truth."

Daumier-Smith's period of guilt over his phony credentials becomes intensified after his flight from the house to covet a secret lunch of hot dogs and "muddy" coffee. In fact, in the packets of the three students assigned to him on his return, the sample of Bambi Kramer's that he calls "unforgettable" is entitled "Forgive Them Their Trespasses," suggestive of Daumier-Smith's pathetic "blue period" as well as the false stance of un-brotherhood to all mankind. After looking into the second packet, the annoyed Daumier-Smith is about to pour out his lifetime of loneliness and abuse, but, thinking better of such a ridiculous gesture to the Yoshotos, he manages to remain seated, having long been "self-trained in taking despair sitting down."

While some critics have noted the incest-theme in "De Daumier-Smith's Blue Period," the story hardly seems to have that narrow a psychological focus when one examines the emphasis given to Sister Irma and especially to her subject matter. First of all, her egolessness is prominent in the story. She encloses no photograph, gives no age, does not even sign her sketches. Even the paper she draws on suggests her Zen-like practicality. Daumier-Smith's conclusion about her picture of Christ being carried to the grave is that it "was . . . an artist's picture, steeped in high, high, organized talent and God knows how many hours of hard work." That Daumier-Smith is on the way toward a religious conversion of his own is once again suggested by Mme. Yoshoto's asking him at dinner if he would not prefer a chair in his room: "I said that the way the floor cushions were set right up against the wall, it gave me a good chance to practice keeping my back straight."

After Daumier-Smith has mailed his first humane letter to another human being, he lies in bed imagining a new vision of the Yoshotos rushing to him to tell him their secret problems (represented by the *moaning* through the wall). He feels he will listen until he can listen to them no longer. He tells us he would "reach down into Mme. Yoshoto's throat, take up her heart in [his] hand and warm it as [he] would a bird."

As Daumier-Smith sweats out the week in anticipation of Sister Irma's answer to his lengthy letter, he actually reaches the lower depths of the Valley of Despair. On his way back from a walk or movie on a Thursday evening (he had mailed his letter Tuesday in the early A.M.), he stops before the orthopedic appliance store. There he is confronted by the wasteland of his former existence, of his life of phoniness: "The thought was forced on me that no matter how coolly or sensibly or gracefully I might one day learn to live my life, I would always at best be a visitor in a garden of enamel urinals and bedpans, with a sightless, wooden dummy-deity standing by in a marked-down rupture truss." While it is true that he has been concerned with the phallic, sexual symbols of his students and even with adjusting his view toward his stepfather, the image of the orthopedic appliances is richly suggestive of the wasteland of phoniness, of sterility, which he has made the determining factors in his early period, his blue phase of the ego aiming for a night at the Ritz, the dandy in his self-conscious clothes, the sophisticate waiting to be tumbled into bed. The only way out of the wasteland, the young narrator imagines, is to free Sister Irma from what he wrongly imagines is her captivity.

The result of his letter, ironically enough, is to release *him*. For though Daumier-Smith writes four letters urging his students to abandon becoming artists, he never mails the second letter he writes to Sister Irma. In it he notes that the worst being an artist can do is to make one slightly "unhappy constantly." At the same time he sees the inevitable merging of the joyous and the despairing in his anecdote about meeting a man without a nose on his way to a lunch in Paris to confront his mother who has just recovered from a serious illness. Daumier-Smith himself, instead of dining in style that night at the Hotel Windsor, goes to a lunch bar, rereads his letters to Sister Irma, and sees its lack of depth. On the way home to revise it, he has the experience of seeing the innocent girl disturbed in her own world of trussing up the store dummy (the noseless man becomes the trussed up dummy). The urinals and bedpans Daumier-Smith discovers after his physical-spiritual flash of insight have become "a shimmery field of exquisite, twice-blessed, enamel flowers." Afterward, he jots down in his diary: "I am giving Sister Irma her freedom to follow her own destiny. Everybody is a nun." That is to say, everyone has his own path of spiritual awareness, however isolated or separated, the talented and untalented, nuns and pornographic artists, dummy-trussers and art teachers. To Daumier-Smith the lesson is a profound one, for he sympathetically reinstates his four art students, returns to his stepfather after the school fails, and instead of criticizing the male and female population, he safely admires the "American Girl in Shorts." Of course, he allows Sister Irma to choose her own life.

"Teddy" is rightly placed as the last of the *Nine Stories*. From Teddy's miraculous powers of perception to the ambiguous ending, the suggestion is made of the importance of the koan affixed to the book. For Teddy's activity, perception, even awareness of death, are beyond the laws of logic—they represent, indeed, "the sound of one hand clapping." And in the same way that we are affected by actions in other stories in which the motivations are beyond the easy laws of logic, we are raised to a higher level of awareness of the real *real* in worlds of tension, contradiction, paradox, humor, love, and squalor.

After "Teddy," Salinger probably reached the point in his development where he was ready to create the Glass family. *Nine Stories* begins with Seymour and ends with Teddy, both of whom have similar characters. And in Daumier-

Smith something of a Buddy, of Salinger himself, emerges, as he does in Sergeant X and even the boy narrator of "The Laughing Man." In these disturbing stories in which the real and unreal, youth and age, love and squalor, and any number of dichotomies either merge or remain separate or isolated, Salinger had perhaps focused his awareness on the necessity for some integrating principle. We believe he had earlier found it in Zen and has continued to develop and to deepen it in the Glass stories.

GERALD ROSEN

A Retrospective Look
at The Catcher in the Rye

Now that over a quarter century has passed since the publication of *The Catcher in the Rye*, it is possible to see the book in the light of the enormous body of writing that has been done on it. There are collections of articles and bibliographies to aid the person who wishes to do this. It is also possible to see the book in the context of Salinger's other work, especially the writings about the Glass family, most of which were published after *Catcher*. These stories reveal themes not immediately apparent in a reading of *Catcher* and stem from a side of Salinger that has been of less importance to his critics than to Salinger himself. I refer to the importance of Eastern thought and religion to Salinger, and of Buddhism in particular, especially the form which we in the West refer to as Zen.

The Zen masters have a saying, "Sometimes we go east, sometimes we go west," and it appears that Salinger, after a brief attempt to "go west" in the American army during World War II, became disillusioned with his native culture and society and turned to a study of Eastern thought. This disillusionment can be seen in Holden's approving remark about his brother D.B.: "My brother D.B. was in the Army for four goddam years. He was in the war, too—he landed on D-Day and all—but I really think he hated the Army worse than the War. . . . He said the Army was practically as full of bastards as the Nazis were." Of course I don't mean to identify Salinger with D.B., but like D.B. Salinger himself participated in the Normandy invasion and his story, "For Esmé—with Love and Squalor," embodies the vision which Holden attributes to D.B.

From *American Quarterly* 29, no. 5 (Winter 1977). © 1977 by Gerald Rosen.

In Buddhism one is asked to give up one's illusions. *Catcher* was given final shape in the postwar period, and it is basically a novel of disillusionment. The radical nature of Salinger's portrayal of disappointment with American society, so much like Twain's in *Huck Finn*, was probably as much of the reason that *Catcher* (like *Huck*) was banned from schools and colleges as were the few curse words around which the battle was publicly fought.

After this novel of the death of belief in America, Salinger turned to wrestling with the problems of Eastern thought in the Glass books. In particular, Franny (who is, in many ways, an older female Holden, suffering from the same alienation-nausea of the seer) and Zooey are faced with the problem of reconciling their interest and training in Eastern thought (embodied in the influence of their brother Seymour upon them) with their deep conditioning and tangled loyalties to Western culture and perceptions and to their personal histories as Jewish-Christian Americans from the Upper West Side of Manhattan. "I was *born* here. I went to *school* here. I've been *run over* here—*twice*, and on the same damn *street*," Zooey lectures Franny (and himself as well).

Since Salinger seemed to achieve instant success with the appearance of *Catcher* in 1951, it is important to remember that he was already in his early thirties by this time, had been publishing stories in slick magazines like the *Saturday Evening Post* for ten years, and had been working on *Catcher* through much of this decade during which time he was studying Buddhism and working on the beginnings of the Glass family saga as well. ("A Perfect Day for Bananafish," and "Down at the Dinghy," were published before *Catcher*).

The Buddha, like most great ancient religious teachers, now exists at the point where the lines of history and legend cross. But as Christmas Humphreys observes in his study of Buddhism, "Legend is often a poetic form of history." A Raja of the Sakya clan (he is sometimes referred to as Sakyamuni—the sage of the Sakyas), the Buddha, according to tradition, was born in what is now Nepal in 563 B.C. His name was Siddhartha Gotama. Raised in a protective, affluent environment, the young prince was shielded from the suffering of the world and not taught to deal with it. The turning point in the story of the Buddha's life occurs when he is confronted with old age, sickness, and death. They so shake him he decides to leave the shelter of his surroundings and the distractions of his involvement in his everyday life in order to wander in the world in search of a guide who will teach him to come to terms with old age, sickness, and death. He doesn't find one, is forced to work out his salvation on his own, persists in his detachment and alienation, has a vision of the truth, and returns to the world out of compassion for his fellow living suffering beings.

I would suggest that, in rough outline, and without the Buddha's final

conscious mature understanding, this is the form of the story of Holden Caulfield. When we first meet Holden in the affluent, protective environment of a
prep school, we are prepared for his lonely journey by immediately being given a
picture of his alienation from the nonseeing groups of people around him.
(Alienation is the negative side of detachment or nonattachment which the
Eastern religions see as a virtue.) Salinger presents us with our first glimpse of
Holden on the day of the big football game. Holden's detachment from the game
is emphasized by having him view the stadium from a distance where the excite-
ment and involvement of the crowd over "the two teams bashing each other all
over the place" appears ridiculous. Holden comments, "The game with Saxon
Hall was supposed to be a very big deal around Pencey. It was the last game of
the year and you were supposed to commit suicide or something if old Pencey
didn't win."

The reference to suicide is not fortuitous for we soon come to see that it is
precisely a continuing preoccupation with death that keeps Holden from partici-
pating in the games of those around him. It prevents him from concentrating on
those activities like day-to-day school chores which we don't ordinarily think of
as games but which, in the presence of death, tend to recede toward the unim-
portance we usually ascribe to games.

And, in fact, just as in the story of the Buddha, it is sickness, old age, and
death, which we the readers, along with Holden, encounter when we begin our
journey through the pages of *The Catcher in the Rye*. We meet sickness and old
age in the form of Mr. Spencer, Holden's teacher:

> The minute I went in, I was sort of sorry I'd come. He was reading
> the *Atlantic Monthly*, and there were pills and medicine all over the
> place, and everything smelled of Vicks Nose Drops. It was pretty
> depressing. I'm not too crazy about sick people, anyway. What made
> it even more depressing, Old Spencer had on this very sad, ratty old
> bathrobe that he was probably born in or something. I don't much
> like to see old guys in their pajamas and bathrobes anyway. Their
> bumpy old chests are always showing. And their legs. Old guys' legs,
> at beaches and places, always look so white and unhairy.

Holden explains to Mr. Spencer that his problem relates to the idea of life
as a game. "He [Dr. Thurmer—the headmaster] just kept talking about life
being a game and all." To which "old" Spencer responds, "Life *is* a game, boy."
Holden agrees with him outwardly, but he tells us, his confidants, "Game my
ass. Some game." At this point Holden believes his objection to life as "a game"
is that it's only fun for the winners. But he has deeper, unconscious objections to

life, since ultimately in life there are no winners, only corpses. And immediately after introducing sickness and old age, Salinger presents us with the third member of the Buddha's problematic triad—death.

Holden, like the young Buddha, is obsessed by death, and by its corollaries, time and change. He has turned Spencer's exam question about ancient Egypt into a short essay which Spencer cannot see as springing out of this obsession: "Modern science would still like to know what the secret ingredients were that the Egyptians used when they wrapped up dead people so that their faces would not rot for innumerable centuries." And Holden flunks, because on this exam, as in his life, no one has ever taught him how to get beyond this primary question, in the shrill light of which all secondary questions are obscured.

From the start, Holden's mind has been filled with images of rot and decay. (Besides "old" Spencer himself, we have also met his rotting bathrobe.) And it is this obsessive concern of Holden's which accounts for the concentration of his narrative upon details of bodily functioning, dirt, and decay—filthy fingernails, mossy teeth, smelly socks, a rusty, filthy razor—which our institutions attempt to repress or deny.

Disgust is our culturally conditioned response to these natural data, and when the book appeared many teachers and reviewers—people who are successfully functioning within the culture's institutional system—did, in fact, respond to the mention of these matters in the text with disgust. Holden is also disturbed by much of this. He, too, has been raised in this culture (many critics have pointed out that he still holds some of the middle-class values he attacks) and he is sickened by their presence. Yet he cannot sweep the evidence of decay and death under the carpet of his mind into his unconscious. He doesn't like what he sees, but he can't help *seeing* it, just as he can't avoid the presence of the central fact of his life, his brother Allie's death, which ultimately sets him off on his quest for an adult guide.

Salinger himself has his present narrator, Buddy Glass, define the artist as seer, and Buddy too seems determined to wrestle openly with death; not only Holden, but the Glass children as well are obsessed by the death of a brother. It was probably a fight against allowing the facts of death and change to get out of his sight and become unconscious that led Salinger to his postwar studies of such philosophies as Taoism and Buddhism which begin with the primary fact of impermanence and change and attempt to teach us to see and accept this central datum of our experience.

Holden has no one to teach him how to cope with death. In a stable culture, one would ordinarily turn to the oldest people for this kind of wisdom. They've been around the longest and presumably would have had the most experience with these matters. But in a rapidly changing culture like ours, the old people and their knowledge appear obsolete to the young. To Holden, the older people he meets are generally all right, but they seem "out of it": "I have this grandmother that's quite lavish with her dough. She doesn't have all her marbles anymore—she's old as hell" and in "old" Spencer's case, "he was a nice old guy that didn't know his ass from his elbow."

Seeking protection himself, Holden is forced to protect the adults he encounters. He forgives Spencer in advance for failing him, writing on his exam, "It is all right with me if you flunk me." Several critics have noted the contradiction between Holden's hatred of phoniness and his lying to Ernest Morrow's mother when he meets her on the train on his way to New York from Pencey. Yet he lies to her to protect her from having to face the fact that "Her son was doubtless the biggest bastard that ever went to Pencey." And it is interesting that when he lies to her about his name, he doesn't do it for the usual reason one lies—to aggrandize oneself—but rather he takes on the name of Rudolph Schmidt, the dorm janitor.

After he fails to get the guidance he needs from his teachers or from the other adults he meets, one would expect Holden to turn to his parents. But in the entire novel, his father never appears and his mother appears once and then only speaks to Phoebe as Holden hides in the closet. The absence of Holden's parents (along with the absence of real religious guidance in the form of a school chaplain or family minister) is so important it amounts to a presence. On the failure of religion, Holden tells us, "my parents are different religions, and all the children in our family are atheists. If you want to know the truth, I can't even stand ministers. . . . They sound so phony when they talk." And, about his family, in the first paragraph Holden explains, "my parents would have about two hemorrhages apiece if I told anything pretty personal about them." Here is the genesis of his hatred of phoniness. His parents live in two worlds: the real world and the world of appearances. The surface does not reveal the underlying reality and Holden has been taught not to talk about what lies beneath. Yet, at times, indirectly, he does. When Phoebe suggests he become a lawyer like their father, he says, "Lawyers are all right, I guess—but it doesn't appeal to me. . . . All you do is make a lot of dough and play golf and play bridge and buy cars and drink martinis and look like a hot-shot." This occurs right after Phoebe asks him to replace their father at her play (the father will be in California on business).

Holden's mother, though well-meaning, won't be of much help either. "She still isn't over my brother Allie yet," and, "She's nervous as hell. Half the time she's up all night smoking cigarettes." Like the other adults, parents can't be relied upon to see, much less give good advice. Holden says of insensitive Stradlater, the secret slob, "he was mostly the kind of a handsome guy that if your parents saw his picture in your Year Book, they'd right away say, 'Who's *this* boy?' "

Holden sorely misses being able to turn to his parents in his time of trouble. He doesn't say this, but he reveals it obliquely in his movie fantasies of being shot by the mob. In the first, he pulls the peak of the hunting cap over his eyes and shouts about being blind. (This is the reverse of the baseball catcher's hat position, in which the peak is *back*, implying the catcher *must* see, and Holden has chosen to be a "catcher.") Then Holden shouts, "Mother darling, everything's getting so *dark* in here," and "Mother darling, give me your *hand*. Why won't you give me your *hand*?" This seems like clowning, but in fact it is a revelation of his terrible anguished isolation from his family. In a later fantasy, Holden reveals, "I didn't want anybody to know I was even wounded. I was *concealing* the fact that I was a wounded sonofabitch." Then he calls Sally and explains the source of his wound: "They got me. Rocky's mob got me." This is clarified three pages later, when he refers to his family at Allie's funeral as "a mob," thereby revealing the source of his wound and the traumatic occasion when he first really felt the pain of it. And he begins to speak of Allie as if he were alive but underground: "I certainly didn't enjoy seeing *him* in that crazy cemetery" [italics added].

So Holden cannot get advice on how to leave the world of childhood from the adults around him. Nor can he find suitable models to emulate. The two Pencey alumni we encounter are Ossenburger, a phony undertaker, and an old guy who appears on Veteran's Day and tells Holden that Pencey will prove to be the best years of his life. This does not increase Holden's hope for the future. And as for Ossenburger, "he started these undertaking parlors all over the country that you could have members of your family buried for about five bucks apiece. . . . You should see old Ossenburger. He probably just shoves them in a sack and dumps them in the river." (Again, Holden can't stay away from the subject of the death of family members and the decay of the corpse. Even when he later goes to the Museum of Art, he winds up in the mummy room explaining about preserving the dead to two boys and then getting sick and "sort of" passing out.)

Holden possesses the necessary but painful gift of the novelist—the intuitive ability to perceive that words are instruments used to create effects and have no necessary attachments to nonverbal reality. So he needs more than even good advice, he needs a living adult, a mature person within the culture who, by his or her living presence, will *demonstrate* a possibility that Holden might achieve if he gives up the nondefined personality of his childhood and accepts a role as a mature member of the society. Holden's brother D.B. who once offered this possibility has sold out to Hollywood which produces images such as the great lover with the violin and the courageous guy with romantic wounds. Since the viewer can't hope to live up to these images, they contribute to making him feel small and uncourageous and add to his wounds. As Holden notes, "The goddam movies. They can ruin you. I'm not kidding." And he isn't. And Mr. Antolini, who gives Holden what might seem to be good advice, cancels any effects his words might have had by his actions and his mode of life.

Americans have always found it difficult to accept limits. Even if the chance to head for the frontier was largely mythic, its significance as myth was its denial of limits in the imaginations of those Americans who were stuck in the East. Of course death is the ultimate limit, and Jessica Mitford has shown to what lengths Americans will go to deny its reality. Institutional roles are limits, too, and Holden, in his extended adolescence, is in the position of one who has been left outside the house of the culture's institutions for too long, and has become taller than the ceiling. Everyone in the house appears to him to be unconscious of the fact that they are stooping to fit inside because this posture has become habitual to them. They have grown into it. Holden is asked to stoop consciously—to enter the house at a time when, so to speak, he has become too tall for it.

In reaction to this, Holden fantasizes a Thoreau-like existence in the country, outside of the limits of institutional roles and of social norms and manners. He tells Sally, "we could drive up to Massachusetts and Vermont, and all around there, see. It's beautiful as hell up there . . . we could live somewhere with a brook and all . . . I could chop all our own wood in the wintertime."

Sally, who has been successfully acculturated, explains to Holden about his obligation to fulfill the traditional male role of husband and provider, and then she promises, "There'll be oodles of marvelous places to go." In responding to Sally, Holden gives us the novel of his future which haunts him and which is one more factor preventing him from accepting an adult role and "growing up" into the society:

> I said no, there wouldn't be marvelous places to go to after I went to college and all. Open your ears. It'd be entirely different. We'd have to go downstairs in elevators with suitcases and stuff. We'd have to phone up everybody and tell 'em goodbye and send 'em postcards from hotels and all. And I'd be working in some office, making a lot of dough, and riding to work in cabs and Madison Avenue buses, and reading newspapers, and playing bridge all the time, and going to the movies.

It is important to note here that Holden's rejection of an adult role is not a case of sour grapes. He believes he *will* succeed and it is the successful life he fears. And this passage, in which he tells Sally to open her eyes and ears, "Open your ears. . . . You don't see what I mean at all," further highlights his desperate isolation. Like the adults, his contemporaries don't see what he sees or hear what he is saying either.

With such a dead-end vision of the trap of adulthood and marriage, it is no wonder that Holden fears initiation into that most adult and most involving and nondetached form of relationship—sex. In a society in which human relationships are infected by marketplace values of competitiveness and surface appearance, and humans are measured in terms of social status and money income, Holden is seeking a deeper, more real relationship with someone—a more human relationship. Holden is against many things, but he isn't nihilistic. "Human" is one of his values, as he reveals comically in his preference for the horse over that sacred American object, the automobile: "A horse is at least *human* for God's sake."

Another positive value of Holden's is that it is wrong to hurt people. He reveals this when he says, in attempting to forgive bores, "They don't hurt anybody, most of them." So Holden is very careful not to use people as a means for his own ends, to try to be certain that he treats each person as a human being and not as a commercial object available for his use in the manner sanctioned by his culture. Yet he is a member of his culture to a degree, so it is not surprising that when he is offered the teenage dream of being indoctrinated into sex in a nonresponsible situation, in which all he has to pay is money, he jumps at the chance, and then, when he is confronted by the human reality of the situation, his tremendous empathy surfaces and he feels sorry for the girl. Of course, Maurice victimizes him here, because Holden allows himself to be victimized by virtually everyone who tries; the culture's emphasis on "winning" in encounters with other people is so threatening to him that he plays it safe by always losing —his scissors to Ackley, his coat to Stradlater, his sweater to James Castle, and so on.

Pure sex, like the myth of rural peace, is a romantic good place Holden is struggling to hold onto in the face of the urban-commercial society determined to pollute both. But Holden's mistrust of sex goes deeper than the merely social level. For Holden, sex is the ultimate involvement in the world; it is the final entry into time. Holden cannot accept change and time is the measure of change. Time is the medium in which change lives. Time is the silent partner of death. And sex is the passageway through which one is seduced into entering time. Salinger makes this connection clear when Sunny, the prostitute, first comes to Holden's room and asks him, three times, whether he has a watch. Of course, he doesn't. He is still a virgin. He has not yet left the timeless world of childhood.

At Pencey, Holden equates sex with time when referring to Stradlater's date with Jane Gallagher. At first, he virtually equates sex with perversion when he calls Stradlater "a very sexy bastard" because of his interest in the details of

Jane's stepfather running around naked in front of her. And then, obsessed with the idea of Stradlater's copulating with Jane, whom Holden remembers as a young girl, he begins to talk of Stradlater's "giving her the time." The fact that this was a popular expression does not reduce the significance of Holden's repeated use of it—rather it generalizes Holden's identification of sex with time.

Thoughts of sex seem to lead Holden to thoughts of death. After the fight with Stradlater over Jane, Ackley asks Holden what the fight was about, and Holden tells us, "I didn't answer him. . . . I almost wished I was dead." In his New York hotel room, when he is thinking about sex and then considers calling Jane at college, an excuse for the late-night call pops into his mind: "I was going to say her aunt had just got killed in a car accident." And after Sunny, the prostitute, leaves his room he begins to talk out loud to his dead brother Allie.

In both Holden's mind and in his culture, besides the link between sex and death there is a connection between sex and aggression, and aggression is an extremely negative quality to Holden. As in his reaction to the culture's emphasis on winning, Holden is so anxious to avoid aggression that he makes himself defenseless. He fights Stradlater, but loses and tells us, "I'd only been in about two fights in my life, and I lost *both* of them. I'm not too tough. I'm a pacifist, if you want to know the truth."

One reason he loses the fight is that he can't make a fist, and it is interesting to note that he injured his fist, and thereby partially rendered himself incapable of aggression, by punching it through a window after Allie died. Aggression, at its extreme, will lead to someone's death and, as Holden comments about the death of Mercutio, "it drives me crazy if somebody gets killed . . . and it's somebody else's fault." Here we have a clue as to why Holden has crippled himself—he has been so shocked by Allie's death that he is afraid to act in the slightest manner that might implicate him in the injustice of it. At bottom, beneath Holden's quarrel with his culture, there is always his quarrel with God whom Holden can't forgive for killing his brother.

Although his swing at Stradlater would seem to violate his anti-aggressive stance, it is in the name of protecting a nonaggressive person that Holden attempts it. What he especially liked about Jane was that she kept her kings in the back row in checkers. This has intrigued the critics, but what it seems to me to represent is a holding back of one's aggressive powers and an unwillingness to enter the competitive game and use them against other people; this is one of Holden's cherished values and, in his own case, his bane as well.

The connection between sex and death in the culture surfaces in the famous scene near the end of the book where Holden attempts to erase the "Fuck You" signs in Phoebe's school. The culture uses the same word for its highest aggressive insult and for its term for sexual intercourse. In the culture's mind and in Holden's, sex is something men *commit* on women and it is clear that this view of sex, built into the culture's language and value system, has poisoned it for Holden.

So here we come full circle: Holden fears aggression because it may lead to death, sex is equated with aggression, and, once again, sex is thus connected with death and with its agent, the grim reaper Time.

In opposition to this vicious circle, Holden dreams of an Edenic world, outside of time, beyond aggression: a world prior to the anxiety caused by the Fall. In his romantic imagination, this world is equated with the prepubescent world of childhood. No one in Holden's world understands natural forces (no adult ever *does* tell him what happens to the ducks in the winter) and puberty resembles death in the way it places man at the mercy of tremendous natural forces which come with one's body and are the price one pays for living in the changing material world. The Hindus, wrestling with these same problems, define this material world as Maya, the veil of illusion, which supposedly keeps one from seeing his ground in the eternal, unchanging, One. The Buddhists see the notion of the unchanging One as one more concept of stability which we manufacture and hold on to to keep from dealing with the reality of change.

Holden holds on to many things to keep from dealing with the reality of change. In the museum, there is glass which keeps things out of time and decay. Holden especially likes the museum for this reason. "The best thing, though, in that museum was that everything always stayed right where it was," and "Certain things should stay the way they are. You ought to be able to stick them in one of those big glass cases and just leave them alone." It is at Allie's funeral that Holden is jolted out of this timeless world that he has seen preserved behind the glass, and, as if in revenge against this fraud, his response is to punch his fist through a window, breaking the glass which has deceived him. Later in the book, beneath the glass in the wall in the Museum of Art, he sees a "Fuck You" scrawled in red crayon and this verbalizes the traumatic insult the timeless world gave him when it broke with Allie's death.

The presence of these "Fuck You" signs in the book points to a crucial difference in attitude between Salinger and his young narrator. The closeness of Salinger and Holden in terms of certain values and aspects of vision is emphasized by Salinger's use of Holden as a first-person narrator. Any distance between them tends to be obscured by Salinger's obvious sympathy for Holden, and by the tone of his writing which succeeds in its scrupulous efforts to get Holden's speech down exactly, creating an intimate effect which is almost like having Holden in the room, telling the reader his own story.

Yet, to ignore the distance between Holden and his creator is to do a disservice to Salinger. In the instance of the "Fuck You" signs, Salinger is doing precisely the opposite of what Holden is attempting to do. Quixotically, Holden

Holden

attempts to erase the "Fuck You" signs, thereby trying to keep children from learning about sex in this misguided (and even aggressive) context. He is trying to be the catcher who keeps children in their Eden before the Fall. Yet Salinger, by *including* these "Fuck You" signs, is actually scrawling them on the walls of his book, forcing the reader to acknowledge their presence and deal with them. At the time the book was published this caused a controversy and was one reason the book was deemed "dirty" by many readers and was taken from libraries and the reading lists of high school courses. Salinger here is not playing the catcher at all, but is asking the reader to grow up and accept the fallen world in which he finds himself.

Interestingly, the readers who attempted to ban the book from libraries and from the schools of their children were acting in exactly the immature manner which causes Holden so much pain and which Salinger is trying to diagnose and prescribe for in the novel. Yet here we see what must be a conflict in Salinger's own mind: after 1947, he has identified himself with the *New Yorker* magazine, publishing almost all his stories in its pages. *Catcher*, however, was not published in the *New Yorker*, and it is clear it couldn't have been published there because of these same "Fuck You" signs.

Brendan Gill tells us, regarding Harold Ross, the founder of the *New Yorker* and its editor at the time *Catcher* was published, that Ross had "a puritanical determination to exclude even the mildest sexual innuendoes." "He said it was his intention to publish nothing that would bring a blush to the cheek of a twelve year old girl. This was a peculiar standard to set for a magazine universally acknowledged to be among the most sophisticated in existence—a magazine that Ross had founded, moreover, with the stipulation that it was not to be edited for the old lady in Dubuque." As for William Shawn, the editor who succeeded Ross and who was in charge during the publication of the Glass stories which came after *Catcher*, Gill comments, "the harshest expletive I ever heard him utter is a whispered, 'Oh, God!' "

Thus, by serving up a fare that includes "Fuck You" signs, Salinger is rebelling against his literary parents at the *New Yorker*, giving them a dish they can't chew and thereby, by implication, putting them in the position of poor immature Holdens, trying to serve as catchers for their readers. And, by the way, perpetuating the same standards of sex and language which are causing Holden so much of his pain. Brendan Gill tells us, "Ross believed in a double standard of language—one for the publicly printed word, the other for private speech."

"Life is suffering." This is the first "Noble Truth" of the Buddha, and it stands like a neon sign over the entrance to Buddhism, acting like a filter that only lets in those who are willing to accept this premise as the price of admission. By the time Holden goes to see his sister Phoebe, one can certainly say that *his* life is suffering in the true Buddhist sense. (Another translation of "suffering" would be "continued irritation" or "anxiety.") The other of the four Buddhist Noble Truths say there is a cause for suffering and a cure. The cause, most briefly termed "desire" or "selfish craving," is said to stem from the failure to accept change (and the failure to deal with sickness, old age, and death) and the concomitant attempt to avoid change by holding on to things, grasping at false possibilities for stability and illusions of permanence. The cure is to let go of desire and selfish craving for ways out of time, be they promised by public gods or private fantasies.

Holden is holding on to many things besides his virginity. He is holding on to his old character patterns which lead him to be unable to let go of saying yes to virtually everything anyone asks him for, and to losing in almost every encounter with other people (especially where money is concerned). He also holds on to objects, such as Allie's glove, and the broken pieces of Phoebe's record (symbolically so like a corpse—the matter is still there, but not the music). He holds on to old opinions as well, such as his (and Allie's) veneration of the kettle drummer at Radio City Music Hall. By avoiding a meeting or a telephone conversation with Jane Gallagher, he holds on to his old image of her which is clearly no longer applicable since she is dating Stradlater; apparently Holden has been defending this image and avoiding her present reality for quite a while since he doesn't even know which school she goes to.

The Buddha said the greatest source of suffering is the belief in a single, continuous, unchanging personality, and the attempt to hold on to it. By not letting go of his old character traits and images of the world, Holden is doing precisely this. Of course, Holden is most strongly holding on to (is most attached to) Allie. When Phoebe challenges Holden to name one thing he likes, he appears to be at a loss for an answer at first, getting stuck on thoughts about James Castle, the boy who committed suicide. Holden is identified with Castle by Castle's having killed himself while wearing Holden's sweater and by Castle's appearing just before Holden on the roll call at school. This carries the implication that Holden may be next in line for Castle's fate. (The fact that Mr. Antolini attempts to help Castle, but is too late, prefigures Holden's experience with Mr. Antolini.) From this image of the dead James Castle, when Phoebe again challenges him, Holden's mind moves back to the image of his dead brother, which he carries with him wherever he goes, and he responds, "I like Allie."

Many people equate Eastern religions with mysticism, and mysticism with pure subjectivity, but Buddhism, at its highest levels, is empirical and asks one merely to be awake to one's real situation and not to believe anything one hasn't experienced. When the Tibetan Buddhist teacher Chogyam Trungpa was talking about finding "a spiritual friend," he was asked by a student, "Is it absolutely necessary that the spiritual friend be a living human being?" to which he replied, "Yes. Any other 'being' with whom you might think yourself communicating would be imaginary."

After Holden says he likes Allie, he immediately turns to the real world and gives us a hint of what will occur at the end of the book at the carrousel. After Phoebe objects, "Allie's *dead*" he adds, "Anyway, I like it now . . . sitting here with you." What Phoebe has done here is to pull Holden out of his obsession with the sorrows of his past and direct his attention to the existential situation he is in at present.

Right after this, Salinger directs our attention to the Buddhist underpinnings of the novel by having Holden inform us about Phoebe, "She was sitting smack in the middle of the bed, outside the covers, with her legs folded like one of those Yogi guys." This is the lotus position of meditation, the traditional posture of the Buddha, and if Holden doesn't know it, Salinger certainly does. To quote Chogyam Trungpa on the Buddhist idea of psychotherapy:

> Once you begin to deal with a person's whole case history, trying to make it relevant to the present, the person begins to feel that he has no escape, that his situation is hopeless, because he cannot undo his past. He feels trapped by his past with no way out. This kind of treatment is extremely unskilled. It is destructive because it hinders involvement with the creative aspect of what is happening now, what is here, right now.

Holden's meeting with Phoebe is the turning point of the book. For the first time he admits, "I just felt good for a change." And the reason he feels good is clear. He is with a person who sees. He tries to lie to her about his getting kicked out of school and she sees through his lie immediately. He tells her, "I'll probably be in Colorado on this ranch," and she responds, "Don't make me laugh. You can't ride a horse." She isn't easy, but she *sees*. And Holden quickly begins to pour out what is bothering him, as if she were a little doctor. When her mother returns with a headache, she prescribes a few aspirin. And she lies to protect Holden, taking the blame for his smoking. These upside-down situations, in which the younger person protects the older ones and gives them advice, are in line with the whole pattern of the book. And the failure of the older people to protect and guide the young not only results in botched initiations like Holden's, it also leads the younger people to try to be their own parents, forcing them to act older than they are by cursing, affecting a false cynicism, lying about their age, drinking, and wearing falsies.

The Zen masters say, "Cold eye, warm heart," and besides seeing, Phoebe is also compassionate. The *Dhammapada* says, "Let us live happily then, we who possess nothing," thereby defining Buddhists. Holden includes Phoebe within this definition when he says, "She says she likes to spread out. That kills me. What's old Phoebe got to spread out? Nothing."

But Phoebe does have a small amount of money, her Christmas money. Eight dollars and sixty-five cents. It isn't much, but it's all she has and she gives it to Holden. And this *act* of compassion breaks through the shell of Holden's fearful isolation: "Then, all of a sudden, I started to cry."

What we have here in miniature, in 1951, is the prescient portrait of an attempt to create a counterculture. The children, unable to connect with the prevailing culture, begin to separate from it and to attempt to care for each other. As the Buddha said, "Brothers and sisters, you have no mother and father to take care of you. If you will not take care of each other, who else, I ask, will do so." We also have the reason for the failure of the counterculture. Holden and Phoebe have charge accounts. The money they give away so freely still comes from their parents and their parents' culture.

Culture is a form of hypnosis and it dies hard. Holden makes one last try to connect. He leaves Phoebe and plays his ace in the hole: Mr. Antolini. Mr. Antolini is full of advice, much of it good, but he is blind to the existential reality of Holden's condition. Once again, when Holden needs a guide, he gets words. They aren't enough. Phoebe remains the only person who has *seen* where he is and who has *acted* truly in his behalf.

So he returns to Phoebe and, in opposition to Antolini's treatment of himself, Holden *watches* the situation and doesn't chase her away, explaining, "I didn't put my hands on her shoulders again or anything because if I had she *really* would have beat it on me. Kids are funny. You have to watch what you're doing." And he accompanies her to the carousel in Central Park where he gives up his desire to be a catcher and his craving for an Edenic world and accepts the world in which he finds himself at present: "The thing with kids is, if they want to grab for the gold ring, you have to let them do it, and not say anything. If they fall off, they fall off, but it's bad if you say anything to them."

In a scene which parallels the one in his parents' apartment when Phoebe gave him her money and his body responded by beginning to cry, here Phoebe gives him a kiss and nature itself seems to respond as it begins to rain. Holden, who has been obsessed with Allie's being out in the rain, stays out in the rain himself, accepts the rain, thereby identifying himself with Allie and Allie's fate, accepting his own death and vulnerability to natural forces. He turns away from what he has lost, letting go of his obsessive hold on the vision of the dead Allie, and turns toward the happiness which comes in seeing what he still has—a living Phoebe, with him, right there in the present. When Holden says, "God, I wish you could've been there," he isn't just talking to us. He is talking to God.

One suspects that this resolution is merely a temporary respite for Holden; that he has a long way to go before he'll be able to extend his acceptance to include the new phonies he meets. But he has survived to tell his story, and in this respect he is more fortunate than Salinger's other "seer," Seymour Glass. After a similar "perfect" encounter with a young girl, Seymour has shot himself through the head.

For the epigraph of his *Nine Stories*, Salinger has chosen the famous Zen koan, "We know the sound of two hands clapping. But what is the sound of one hand clapping?" A koan has no "right" answer. A particular koan is given to a particular student to see from many sides and learn from, but ultimately it is something that, however fascinating, must be let go of. I would suggest that this first Glass story, "A Perfect Day for Bananafish," is a kind of koan, one whose meaning the Glass children will be meditating on and wrestling with for years to come. Ultimately, the problems faced by Holden and the Glass children have no "answer" that *we* can hold on to. But we must be careful not to ask Salinger or anyone else to provide us with this illusory "answer." As Salinger certainly knows, tradition has it that when the Buddha was dying he was asked for one final piece of advice and he replied, "Work out your own salvation with diligence."

JOHN WENKE

Sergeant X, Esmé,
and the Meaning of Words

She went on to say that she wanted all *her children to absorb the* meaning
of the words they sang, not just mouth *them, like silly-billy parrots.*
— "For Esmé—with Love and Squalor"

During a time when many writers are reconsidered, reconstructed, rediscovered, or revisited, the last ten years have been remarkable for the apparent decline of critical interest in J. D. Salinger. Over the last two decades, Salinger has had so little to say that his commentators, once a spirited and argumentative group, seem to have followed the lead of the master and have become, for the most part, silent. Many readers of Salinger's work vacillate regularly between the conviction that he is in New Hampshire composing masterpiece after masterpiece but refusing to publish, and the less fantastic, more sobering suspicion that he is simply growing vegetables and repeating the Jesus Prayer. Nevertheless, the small body of fiction remains as a cryptic reminder of a significant contemporary writer who has adopted an enigmatic public silence. While any resolution to the mystery of Salinger's silence must remain elusive for the moment, certain implications in his best short story may go some way in accounting for the retreat, without having to construe it as an outgrowth of his later preoccupation with Zen. His continuing silence may well have evolved from the conviction that deeply felt human emotions need no expression—a position implied by the successful aesthetic resolution of "For Esmé—with Love and Squalor."

In the fifties and sixties, the critical debate over "For Esmé" focused on various aspects of love and squalor as they relate to the narrator (Sergeant X), Esmé, Charles, and Clay (Corporal Z). While the story does in fact dramatize

From *Studies in Short Fiction* 18, no. 3 (Summer 1981). © 1981 by Newberry College.

Sergeant X's redemption from an emotional and physical breakdown through the transformative powers of love, the narrative also—and most importantly—examines the reasons why forms of expression—whether conversational, literary, or epistolary, to name a few—either have meaning and propagate love, or lack meaning and impede emotional stability. For Salinger, failures of language advance the horror, vacuity, and despair of modern life. Throughout the narrative, Salinger reflects his concern with exploring the validity of language by persistently alluding to such indirect, constructed modes of discourse as letters, books, or inscriptions. Failed forms of communication seem to be everywhere, the most notable of which is Sergeant X's illegible response to a Nazi woman's inscription, "Dear God, life is hell," in Goebbels' "Die Zeit Ohne Beispiel." In "For Esmé" letters, books, conversations, and inscriptions usually create (or continue) rather than alleviate the emotional vacuum in which most of the characters live. Nowhere else in Salinger's fiction does he more intensely present the paradox and dilemma of modern man: to speak is not to express; to employ forms of expression is often to evade the difficulties of significant communication. Beneath the most obvious progression of action and theme in "For Esmé" resides the moral basis for Salinger's art which indicates why, at the end of the story, two successful acts of communication are completed, while, throughout most of the story itself, dramatizing the reasons why most acts of expression fail.

In a story replete with failed forms of communication, one must consider why Esmé's saving letter has such a positive effect, and how it has anything to do with the rest of the narrative as well as Salinger's later and continuing silence. These issues can be explored by first examining the story's many human relationships. In "For Esmé," it is difficult to find many instances of love based on sympathetic understanding and shared experiences. Debased, destructive relationships predominate and are manifested most vividly through the narrator's relation to his wife and mother-in-law, his fellow soldiers in camp, and Clay and Loretta. Underlying these failures of love and sympathy reside the breakdown and deterioration of the power of language to express true feeling.

At the outset of the story, Salinger satirizes the mundane actualities and practical considerations of postwar America. The narrator's wife, a "breathtakingly levelheaded girl," and the impending visit of Mother Grencher, who, at fifty-eight, is "not getting any younger," detain him from going to Esmé's wedding. Apparently, the wife has little sense of Esmé's importance to her husband, and the narrator, while wryly undercutting his wife's practicality, does not seem capable of acting against her wishes. His tongue seems to be firmly in cheek as he ticks off the reasons why the proposed trip need not be made. In fact, he seems to be repeating the strictures as they were dictated to him. Such a failure marks a continuation of the "stale letters" the narrator received during the war.

Reports on the service at Schrafft's and requests for cashmere yarn, like the prohibition against attending the wedding, extend selfish interests, while, at the same time, they evidence little concern for the narrator's needs.

His difficulties with these two women signal a problem that appears elsewhere in other forms—the sterility of conventional relationships. There is, for example, no fellowship among the troops at the training camp. The absence of community is predicated upon the failure of language. These letter-writing types, living in a self-imposed limbo, pen their letters in order to avoid human contact. The narrator, in particular, uses forms of expression to distance himself from those around him; he escapes, for example, into the books which he carries about in his gas mask container. His general disgust with experience appears most clearly through his use of cliché. Such tired language mocks the traditional bravado associated with war, and it exploits the disparity between fresh rhetorical assessments and degraded, sterile statements:

> I remember standing at an end window of our Quonset hut for a very long time, looking out at the slanting, dreary rain, my trigger finger itching imperceptibly, if at all. I could hear behind my back the uncomradely scratching of many fountain pens on many sheets of V-mail paper. Abruptly, with nothing special in mind, I came away from the window and put on my raincoat, cashmere muffler, galoshes, woolen gloves, and overseas cap. . . . Then, after synchronizing my wristwatch with the clock in the latrine, I walked down the long, wet cobblestone hill into town. I ignored the flashes of lightning all around me. They either had your number on them or they didn't.

Just as the narrator's exploitation of cliché reflects the general bleakness of military life, so also does the perversion of romantic language point to significant failures in conventional ways of ordering experience. The relationship between Clay and Loretta is maintained through meaningless forms which make their courtship an exercise in mutual self-delusion. Intending to marry "at their earliest convenience," she writes to him "fairly regularly, from a paradise of triple exclamation points and inaccurate observations." Their relationship epitomizes the way in which language in "For Esmé" fails to communicate deep feeling, but instead propagates the antithesis of love—squalor. Salinger implies that their lack of self-awareness and moral introspection is not merely contemptible, but is actually a succinct embodiment of those very forces of insensitivity and self-justification which create and sustain the absurdity of war. Clay revels in the delusion that temporary insanity, rather than sadism, made him shoot a cat.

In "For Esmé—with Love and Squalor," such characters as the narrator's wife and mother-in-law, Clay and Loretta, are impervious to the existential ravage inflicted by the war; others, like the soldiers in the camp and the narrator himself, perceive the bleakness of experience but can do little or nothing to overcome it or escape from it. By escaping into letter-writing, into books, or by adopting a cynical attitude, they repudiate the possibility of community and compound their isolation through acts of quiet desperation.

Nonetheless, the very fact that the story is even told in the first place suggests that there is a way to be immersed in squalor, recognize it as such, and eventually overcome it. "For Esmé" depicts extreme human misery, the suffering of being unable to love, at the same time that the narrator's very capacity to tell his story provides the completion of the psychological therapy which began when he read Esmé's letter and fell asleep. In telling the story, the narrator has clearly achieved a balance in his life, which, at the outset of the story, is implied by his good-natured, if ironic, tone. Unlike all other attempts to communicate, Esmé's letter and the process of telling the tale itself come directly out of the forces underlying their personal encounter in the Devon tearoom and possess a basis in love which is founded upon similar recognitions of the effect of squalor on the other. These acts of communication are not spontaneous emanations, but come out of periods of retrospection and consolidation during which each perceives the import of that "strangely emotional" time which they spent together. Esmé's decision to send X her father's watch could not have been hasty or gratuitous. A six-year period of recovery precedes the composition of the narrator's "squalid and moving" story. For Salinger, it seems, meaningful human expression must be founded on authentic emotions which evolve into a sympathetic comprehension of another's individual needs. Forms of expression are, in themselves, neutral; they become meaningful or parodic to the extent that love or squalor resides at the heart of the relationship. The love that Salinger affirms in "For Esmé" does not depend on words, but on an emotional inner transformation which must be understood and assimilated before it can be expressed. Forms of expression cannot create love, as Clay and Loretta try to do through letters, but only express what has mysteriously been there from the start. In "For Esmé," we encounter a significant moment in Salinger's fiction, a moment during which ineffable emotional states find expression in literary forms.

Given what has been argued thus far, it would be helpful to examine just how the conversation between the narrator and Esmé in the tearoom relates to his epiphany at the conclusion of the story. Basically, we shall see how their conversation offers vital insights into the psychological needs of each character, even though the apparent surface meaning of their words does not seem to indicate the formation of a deep and lasting bond of love.

For both the narrator and Esmé, language does not directly mirror their true inner states, but instead provides a defense, a kind of mask from behind which the suffering self cryptically speaks. The narrator adopts a protective cynicism, which largely accounts for the strange shiftings of tone and point of view evident throughout the meeting. Esmé's famous malaprops and inflated diction are the basic elements with which she constructs her persona. For both characters, language offers a way to cover up their psychological fragility, insecurity, and acute self-consciousness, even though some very minor actions help to reflect most clearly the tenuousness of their respective poses. The narrator, for example, smiles but is careful to hide his "coalblack filling," while Esmé's fingernails are bitten to the quick and her tendency to keep touching her hair belies her posture of self-assurance.

It is probably not necessary to detail Esmé's strained attempts to appear older, more mature, self-possessed. Nonetheless, a brief look at the way the narrative voice oscillates between sarcasm and sincerity will suggest how language covers up, rather than directly reflects, the true state of the narrator's being. When watching the choir practice, the narrator emanates a glib, sardonic attitude: "Their voices were melodious and unsentimental, almost to the point where a somewhat more denominational man than myself might, without straining, have experienced levitation." His deflation of the choir is offset a few lines later by a genuine admiration for Esmé's voice: "Her voice was distinctly separate from the other children's voices, and not just because she was seated nearest me. It had the best upper register, the sweetest-sounding, the surest, and it automatically led the way." During their conversation itself, his tone and emotional state continue to fluctuate between sarcasm and sincerity. When asked whether he attends that "secret Intelligence school on the hill," he notes that he is "as security-minded as the next one" and therefore tells Esmé that he is "visiting Devonshire for my health." Shortly thereafter, the narrator admits that he is glad she came over, since he "*had* been feeling lonely."

Generally, their conversation is amiable, congenial, interesting, and leaves the narrator pondering the "strangely emotional" moment which the departure of Charles and Esmé creates. On the surface, this meeting does not seem to satisfactorily explain Esmé's capacity to overwhelm X with love at the end of the story. On the basis of the language and action alone, one may be inclined to view Leslie Fiedler's nearly blasphemous assertion that "For Esmé" is "a popular little tearjerker" with some sympathy. The conversation, however, helps to suggest some basic facts about each character: the narrator is greatly in need of emotional sustenance; Esmé, midway between childhood and adulthood, must cope with the pain of having lost both parents at the same time that she must bear the responsibility of taking care of her brother. Their conversation implies, but does not explicitly record, the extent of each character's emotional reaction.

Ultimately, one must perceive that, underlying the words and actions of this scene, some kind of inscrutable magnetism touches the narrator and Esmé, which evolves from an instinctual and unconscious sense that each possesses what the other most deeply needs. In light of the subsequent action, it can be argued that Esmé senses in the narrator the capacity to represent a surrogate father, while the narrator, disgusted by the petty actualities of stale middle-class life and the bleak atmosphere among the letter-writing types, senses in Esmé a saving balance between the "silly-billy" innocence of children and the squalor of adulthood. In the tearoom, neither character is fully aware of the implications of this "strangely emotional moment." But as time passes, each retrospectively achieves insight into the nature of their love, and the capacity to respond is manifested by the creation of meaningful forms of expression. Only later, with Esmé's letter and the loan of her father's watch, do we find that she fully recognizes the import of the meeting. For the narrator, the recitation of the story—the artistic process—fulfills his promise to write Esmé a story both "squalid and moving."

Salinger denies us a view of the psychological process which prompts Esmé to forward her father's watch. We do, however, witness X's emergence from a hell characterized by explicit failures of language to communicate love. While his inability to read, write, or think clearly is a result of the "suffering of being unable to love," human contact causes even further deterioration. His conversation with Clay and the letter from his brother structurally parallel X's earlier conversation with Esmé and the letter he later opens from Esmé. Here, however, these forms of communication perform exactly the opposite office, indicating that language, not founded on love and a sympathetic comprehension of another's condition, expresses negation and advances alienation. Because of his insensitivity, Clay cannot comprehend the extent and cause of X's emotional deterioration. Clay does not even understand why X sarcastically interprets Clay's reasons for killing "that pussycat in as manly a way as anybody could've under the circumstances." The conversation culminates in X's nausea, which follows Clay's most ironic failure to perceive the meaning of X's words:

> "That cat was a spy. You *had* to take a pot shot at it. It was a
> very clever German midget dressed up in a cheap fur coat. So there
> was absolutely nothing brutal, or cruel, or dirty, or even—"
> "God damn it!" Clay said, his lips thinned. "Can't you ever be
> *sincere?*"
> X suddenly felt sick, and he swung around in his chair and grabbed
> the wastebasket—just in time.

This is undoubtedly the same wastebasket which holds the torn remnants of his brother's request for souvenirs, the accoutrements of the very war which threatens to destroy X's being. His brother's letter was probably sent in the unquestioned belief that the Sergeant receiving the letter would be the same one who left home. This Sergeant, however, has gone through a revolution of consciousness, profoundly altering his relation to home, self, and society. Americans back home like X's wife, mother-in-law, and brother inhabit a spatial, experiential, and psychological world which is entirely foreign to X's life. They have no way to comprehend the waste and horror which X has seen. Thus, his brother's letter accentuates distance, fails to provide relief, and moves X closer to an absolute loss of reason.

Neither callous letter, nor talking to Clay about Loretta, nor listening to Bob Hope on the radio can help X to recover his faculties. Instead, he needs personal contact with someone who has a sensitive understanding of the way war can destroy one's being. Like X, Esmé has been ravaged by the war and, emotionally, her experiences and problems are similar to the Sergeant's: she has been stripped of her former source of coherence, order, and love through the death of her parents; Sergeant X's former way of ordering experience no longer pertains to his life; both need to reconstruct their lives after being "wounded" by the war. By chance, X opens Esmé's letter and receives help from the only available source. The act of reading the letter stuns him, touching off an awareness of the significance of their meeting in the tearoom. The letter and the loan of her father's watch spring from Esmé's deep desire to express love. It is not so much the letter's stilted words or the statistics which affect X; instead, it is his deeply felt, overwhelming experience of Esmé's love which begins his cure by inducing sleep.

"For Esmé" reflects the power of language to communicate love. Here, Salinger successfully mediates between silence and sentimentality by presenting two instances of expression—Esmé's letter to the narrator and the narrator's story "for Esmé"—which evolve from each character's comprehension of the meaning of love. These forms of expression represent moral and aesthetic resolutions to the problems of human communication permeating the narrative. Unlike the endings of many classic American tales, the conclusion of "For Esmé—with Love and Squalor" fulfills the process of self-recovery rather than simply bringing the hero to a point at which he either has nowhere to go or is *about* to make use of what he has learned. "For Esmé" has closure at the same time that it suggests how the narrator will live within society, even though his experiences have taught him the inherent failure of conventional society. On the one hand, the ending of the story completes the process of therapy which began with the discovery of Esmé's letter, fulfills the promise to write her a story, and completes the office of symbolic father. As Ihab Hassan notes, the story can be looked at as a "modern epithalamium." It is also a wedding gift, a parting gesture of love from father to daughter. On the other hand, the narrator has managed to gain a balanced perspective; he has found a way to avoid paralyzing isolation and survive with good humor even though living within a world dominated by the likes of his wife and mother-in-law. Even though he may be impeded from acting as he would like, he still has his art.

Communication is difficult within such a world, but possible. Salinger dramatizes this difficulty by crowding his world with people who are not so much malicious as unconscious. The best one can say about Clay, for example, is that he tries to help X. But like most characters in Salinger's fiction, Clay is impeded by his utter incapacity to transcend the values which he holds sacred and never questions. Thus, one response to the horror which threatens civilization resides in accommodating oneself completely to the stereotypical conventionalities of middle-class existence—the world of Saks, cashmere, convenient marriages, college psychology courses, war souvenirs, and complacent acceptance of army bureaucracy. But in presenting two successful expressions of love, Salinger offers an optimistic answer to the implied question: How can one respond to the void after confronting, in Esmé's words, "a method of existence that is ridiculous to say the least?"

Nevertheless, "For Esmé" presents the early signs in Salinger of his apparent acceptance of silence, not as a negative or cowardly retreat from the literary field, as some of his detractors would have it, but as a positive, implicit recognition of emotions that are in themselves meaningful and therefore need no expression. This story is so interesting because it confronts the difficulty of significant human communication at a time when he still seemed to believe in writing (or at least publishing). "For Esmé—with Love and Squalor" is indeed a high point in Salinger's art for many of the reasons his other commentators have noted. Most notably, though, it addresses one of the central problems of Salinger's fiction in particular and modern literature in general—the problem of finding valid forms of communication—at the same time that the story suggests that love is the force which animates expression. In a story in which love ultimately triumphs, the relationship between the narrator and Esmé embodies a beautiful, if tenuous, example of how individuals might pass through squalor to love, achieving meaningful, redemptive expression, even though the successful uses of language are a constant reminder of its general failure.

DENNIS L. O'CONNOR

J. D. Salinger's Religious Pluralism: The Example of "Raise High the Roof Beam, Carpenters"

As a writer with serious religious concerns, J. D. Salinger belongs to a venerable American tradition dating from the time of Emerson and the transcendentalists. In the company of such artists as Thoreau, Whitman, Eliot, Ginsberg, Gary Snyder, and Thomas Merton, Salinger has responded deeply to a variety of Eastern spiritualities. Although his writings appeal to a variety of audiences on several levels, most American critics of his work have fastened on psychological or sociological questions. Even so, a few voices have responded to the religious dimensions of his art. Some problems arose, however, when certain sympathetic critics analyzed his fiction in light of these religious interests. These problems were twofold: (1) his flawless Manhattanese seemed perfectly obvious and in no need of further study; and (2) the Glass family tales betrayed an "increasing" absorption in unfamiliar Oriental ideas. Whereas few critics troubled to probe Salinger's colloquial diction (thereby ignoring the subtle shifts in meaning reminiscent of Chekhov), even fewer sought to elucidate his Orientalism (usually reduced to Zen) in relation to his narrative art.

To solve this critical impasse, I propose to examine certain religious dimensions of Salinger's fiction by focusing on "Raise High the Roof Beam, Carpenters," the first of his Glass family chronicles. Although published twenty-five years ago in the New Yorker, its meaning remains largely unexplored. My argument has three parts. First, I will explicate the Taoist text of Lieh-tzu which introduces the story and relate it to the subsequent narrative. Second, I will analyze the three characters (Kao, Seymour, and the nameless old man) who constitute a Taoist fellowship and reveal the riches of Salinger's religious art.

From The Southern Review 20, no. 2 (April 1984). © 1984 by Dennis L. O'Connor.

Third, I will demonstrate Salinger's religious pluralism in terms of his complementary use of Taoist, Buddhist, and Christian thought.

Salinger himself suggests the direction of this study when he has Buddy Glass explain his religious pluralism. "Would it be out of order," Buddy asks, "for me to say that both Seymour's and my roots in Eastern philosophy—if I may hesitatingly call them 'roots'—were, are, planted in the New and Old Testament, Advaita Vedanta, and classical Taoism?" Indeed, I will argue, it is *not* out of order, it *is* the order, the very soul of his writing. "Seymour once said that all we do our whole lives is go from one piece of Holy Ground to the next. Is he *never* wrong?" The climactic affirmation of Seymour, which Buddy recalls at the end of his long struggle, is, I believe, the quintessence of Salinger's religious vision and the warrant for this study. His vision entails a reverence for language, a delight in everyday speech which ceaselessly reveals the very depths of our lives. And so I will examine Salinger's language in relation to the "piece of Holy Ground" disclosed in "Raise High."

I

This Glass family chronicle begins curiously. Buddy Glass, Salinger's first person narrator, sets the stage by recounting in 1955 an event from 1934, when his sister Franny, ten months old, spent the night with him and Seymour during a "siege" of the mumps. Awakened by Franny's crying, Buddy finds Seymour soothing his sister by reading aloud a Taoist tale. When Buddy objects that she's only an infant, Seymour replies, "They have ears. They can hear." By alluding to a biblical injunction about childlike reception of the word of God, Seymour stresses the seriousness of his action, the sacredness of the Taoist text, and the religious pluralism that characterizes Salinger's fiction.

In complementary distinction to the biblical emphasis upon hearing and responding to God's word, this Taoist tale stresses spiritual insight and the difference between routine adult misperception and childlike vision. The selection offered without citation is from Lionel Giles's translation, *Taoist Teachings from the Book of Lieh-tzu*, and forms part of the eighth and final chapter, "Explaining Conjunctions." Salinger quotes this tale verbatim because, with Seymour's diary, it illumines his entire narrative. I will now try to explicate the relation between these two works by exploring the Taoist background and Salinger's unique appropriation of it in his story.

In Lieh-tzu's parable, when Duke Mu asked Po Lo, his aged judge of horses, to recommend a worthy successor, he replied: "A good horse can be picked out by its general build and appearance. But the superlative horse—one that raises no dust and leaves no tracks—is something evanescent and fleeting, elusive as thin air . . . my sons can tell a good horse when they see one, but they cannot tell a superlative horse." He then recommended Chiu-fang Kao, "a hawker of fuel and vegetables." Dispatched to a remote region for such a steed, Kao reported after three months that he had found one. And, upon demand, he described it as a dun-colored mare. But when a coal black stallion arrived, Duke Mu complained to Po Lo that Kao could not even distinguish color and sex. Delighted, Po Lo exclaimed, "Ah, then he is worth ten thousand of me. . . . Kao keeps in mind the spiritual mechanism. In making sure of the essential, he forgets the homely details; intent on the inward qualities, he loses sight of the external . . . he has it within him to judge something better than horses." Drawing a parallel between Kao and Seymour, Buddy laments his brother's absence (through suicide): "Since the bridegroom's retirement from the scene, I haven't been able to think of anybody whom I'd care to send out to look for horses in his stead."

Lieh-tzu's parable, like the earlier works of Lao-tzu and Chuang-tzu, envisions a man living in the *Tao*, the Heavenly Way of perfect freedom and harmony with nature, where one loses self-consciousness and becomes as soft as water, as yielding as a woman, as free as a child, as unformed as a block of wood. Entering this emptiness without limit, form, or name, one loses any previous identity as a separate self. Now emptied of this false self (the acquisitive empirical ego with all its desires and illusions—the "old man" in St. Paul's sense), the person opens up to the Way which embraces all of being and non-being. Thus, a man "lost in *Tao*" has the spiritual freedom to envision the superlative horse, for only a visionary would ignore color and sex (shorthand for all human criteria) to judge things in the light of Tao. Kao sees deeply, while Duke Mu and everyone lost in the obvious, miss what matters. The horse actually symbolizes one's deepest self dwelling in Tao, for the steed's elusiveness suggests the Way's characteristic transcendence of all language and objectification. According to the *Tao Te Ching* of Lao-tzu, "There are ways but the Way is uncharted . . . nameless indeed in the source of creation. . . . The secret waits for the insight of eyes unclouded by longing; those . . . bound by desire see only the outward container." Graced with such insight, Kao glimpses his innermost heart, the evanescent superlative horse of the human spirit. His vision, born of inward stillness that "raises no dust and leaves no tracks," recalls Lao-tzu's poetic description of the Tao's simplicity and lightness: "A good runner leaves no tracks. . . . A good knot is tied without rope and cannot be loosed."

II

Buddy's deceptively casual statement about Seymour's "retirement" leaving him unable "to think of anybody whom I'd care to send out to look for horses in his stead" introduces the pivotal Taoist fellowship of Kao, Seymour, and the nameless old man who befriends the narrator on his brother's wedding day. These three visionaries suggest the religious depth which interprets and tempers Buddy's narrative, whose central themes include true versus false vision; and oppressive societal demands for "normalcy" versus the uncategorical way of the artist-seer living in the Tao.

Having considered Kao in light of Lieh-tzu's parable, we turn now to Seymour Glass, the true subject of Buddy's narrative and the corrective lens through which we understand the brothers. Avoiding common classifications and misjudgments, Seymour, like Kao, lives in the Heavenly Way. Chuang-tzu's description of the Man of Tao suggests Seymour's own personality:

> The non-action of the wise man is not inaction . . . .
> The sage is quiet because he is not moved . . . .
> Still water is like glass.
> The heart of the wise man is tranquil.
> It is the mirror of heaven and earth
> The glass of everything.
> Emptiness, stillness, tranquility, tastelessness,
> Silence, non-action: this is the level of heaven and earth
> This is the perfect Tao. Wise men find here
> Their resting place.
> Resting they are empty.

By resting in the Tao, Seymour radiates the truth of his name: seeing more, he acts in a nonintervening way until his presence is as clear as glass. In Taoist terms, this action is *wu-wei*, literally "nondoing," that is, he acts naturally, inconspicuously, and spontaneously. Thus, his actions seem formless and empty, as aimless and "unproductive" as passing clouds or rain. In fact, the Chinese use water, the epitome of wu-wei's dynamic, to symbolize the gracious humility of Tao:

> The highest goodness, water-like,
> Does good to everything and goes
> Unmurmuring to places men despise;
> But so, is close in nature to the Way.

This imagery recalls the biblical image of rain falling on the just and unjust as a sign of God's all-inclusive mercy.

Seymour's "water-like," nonjudgmental wu-wei informs his relationship to his bride and her family. A diary entry, written before the wedding, exemplifies his understanding acceptance of Muriel Fedder and her parents:

> The familiarity between Muriel and her mother struck me as being
> so beautiful when we were all sitting in the living room. They know

each other's weaknesses . . . and pick at them with their eyes. . . .
When they argue, there can be no danger of a permanent rift, because they're Mother and Daughter. A terrible and beautiful phenomenon to watch. Yet there are times . . . I wish Mr. Fedder were
more conversationally active. Sometimes I feel I need him. Sometimes, in fact, when I come in the front door, it's like entering a kind
of untidy, secular, two-woman convent. Sometimes when I leave, I
have a peculiar feeling that both M. and her mother have stuffed my
pockets with little bottles and tubes containing lipstick, rouge, hair
nets, deodorants, and so on. I feel overwhelmingly grateful to them,
but I don't know what to do with their invisible gifts.

Where Buddy reviles his enemies and then withdraws into self-pity, Seymour
accepts without winking or accusation. He senses that Mr. Fedder is castrated,
that masculinity has no chance in this "two-woman convent," and that mother
and daughter are set on domesticating him as well. Indeed, his imagining their
stuffing him with "feminine notions," the clichés and accoutrements of their
derivative identities, indicates his awareness of their effort to appropriate his
manhood. This "terrible and beautiful phenomenon" would make him "normal," that is, one of them, by pressuring him into psychoanalysis, a treatment
that promises psychic mutilation for the poet. Nevertheless, despite their efforts
to "overhaul" him, he remains happy and open.

Seymour's mysterious equanimity, which neither Buddy, nor Muriel, nor
Mrs. Fedder, nor apparently the majority of Salinger's critics can understand,
makes sense from a Taoist perspective. In fact, Salinger offers a Taoist clue in the
first diary entry, where Seymour contrasts his tranquility with the distress of his
fellow soldiers fainting from the cold. "I have no circulation, no pulse. Immobility
is my home. The tempo of 'the Star-Spangled Banner' and I are in perfect
understanding. To me, its rhythm is a romantic waltz." This serenity recalls
Lieh-tzu's meditation on the sage: "holding fast to his purest energies . . . he will
unify his nature . . . until he penetrates to the place where things are created. If
you can be like this, the Heaven inside you will keep its integrity, the spirit inside
you will have no flaws . . . the sage hides himself in Heaven, therefore no thing
can harm him." Living in the Way, Seymour need not choose between military
and romantic music. As Lieh-tzu says, "the man . . . in harmony is absolutely the
same as other things, and no thing succeeds in wounding or obstructing him."
Precisely because Seymour dwells in the Tao, he is unrushed, unfatigued, tranquil
in the emptiness of wu-wei which entails "freedom from the accretions of desire
and the influence of the senses." Thus, his peace presupposes a flexible detachment that overcomes all obstacles. Huai-nan-tzu aptly described those resting in
wu-wei as possessing "a yielding mind; nevertheless their work is invincible."

If Taoist thought clarifies Seymour's serenity, it also explains his apparent "formlessness." Buddy's reference to him in "Seymour", as a "Formless Bastard," provides another Taoist clue. As Chuang-tzu observes, "[the True Master] can act—that is certain. Yet I cannot see his form. He has identity but no form." If Seymour eludes "normal," rational categories, neither defense nor attack makes any difference. Thus Chuang-tzu comments that "to men such as these [who dwell in the Way], how could there be any question of putting life first or death last? . . . Idly they roam beyond the dust and dirt: they wander free and easy in the service of inaction [*wu-wei*]. Why should they fret about the ceremonies of the vulgar world. . . ?" This freedom from competition and self-aggrandizement (the "dust and dirt" of appetitive striving) transforms Seymour's mind into a polished mirror whose emptiness effortlessly reflects what it sees and is. Such inner clarity manifests itself in contemplative detachment, what the eleventh-century Taoist painter, Mi Yu-jen, called "the wisdom of the eye." "When we reach maturity in painting," he wrote, "we are not attached to the mundane world. . . . Whenever in the quiet of my room with my legs crossed I sit silently then I feel that I float up and down with the blue sky, vast and silent." Such intuition of "the interfusion of the self with the universe" and the harmony of form and formlessness (the sky, like an uncarved block or running water, is a Taoist symbol of formlessness), being and nonbeing (wu), characterizes wu-wei. In his recent study, *Creativity and Taoism*, Chang Chung-yuan argues that wu-wei "does not mean quiescence after action has ceased, but quiescence forever in action." Thus, Seymour's own waterlike formlessness is dynamic, but, like his full name, it serves as a mirror and a lens to quietly reflect and focus the flowing world. Chuang-tzu's meditation on formlessness unfolds this inner richness. According to this greatest of Chinese philosophers, "man alone is more than an object. Though, like objects, he has form and semblance, he is not limited to form. He is more. He can attain to formlessness. When he is beyond form and semblance, beyond 'this' and 'that' . . . where is the conflict? He will rest in his eternal place which is no-place. He will be hidden in his own unfathomable secret. His vitality, his power hide in secret Tao."

Before discussing the third member of the Taoist fellowship, the childlike nameless one who befriends Buddy, I should briefly mention two other Glass family members who embody this Taoist ideal of yielding formlessness. As little children Franny and Zooey manifest the freedom of the Heavenly Way while appearing on the radio program called "It's a Wise Child." The first incident, which Boo Boo mentions in her letter to Buddy, involves Franny's recollecting how "she used to fly all around the apartment when she was four and no one was home." Since Buddy prefaced his narrative with Franny's claim that she remembers hearing Lieh-tzu's parable, it seems fitting that she should imitate the man who claimed "my mind concentrated and my body relaxed . . . I drifted with the wind East or West, like a leaf . . . and never knew whether it was the wind that rode me or I that rode the wind." Chuang-tzu uses this essential emptiness, formlessness, and sameness of the Tao to characterize a child. The second incident concerns Zooey's response to the questions of sameness. "He said it would be very nice to come home and be in the wrong house. To eat dinner with the wrong people by mistake, sleep in the wrong bed by mistake, and kiss everybody goodbye in the morning thinking they were your own family. He said he even wished everybody in the world looked exactly alike. He said you'd keep thinking everybody you met was your wife or your mother or father, and people would always be throwing their arms around each other wherever they went." Aside from its Taoist qualities of harmony, prereflective unity, and wu-wei, Zooey's vision also contains eschatological, messianic, and eucharistic implications. In the biblical vision of the heavenly Jerusalem, when Christ will be all in all at the end of time, we shall see God face to face and know him even as we ourselves are known. Released from the bonds of sin and death, we will live in our glorified risen bodies as Jesus's brothers and sisters, the flesh and blood of his mystical body at last whole and harmonious. Within this eucharistic fellowship of unending love, we will be God's true image and likeness, at once profoundly ourselves and perfectly intimate with every other being in his creation.

Placing Zooey's religious vision in the context of Seymour's evening with the Fedders, Salinger emphasizes its relation to the Vedantic passage which concludes Seymour's diary. "I've been reading a miscellany of Vedanta all day. Marriage partners are to serve each other. Elevate, help, teach, strengthen each other, but above all *serve*. Raise their children honorably, lovingly, and with detachment. A child is a guest in the house, to be loved and respected—never possessed, since he belongs to God." Harmonizing with both the gospel teaching about welcoming children in the name of Jesus and his heavenly Father and the resulting Christian monastic custom of receiving each guest as another Christ, this Vedantic injunction stresses compassionate service that coincides with Taoist reverence for creation and childlike spontaneity.

Like Kao and Seymour, the third member of the Taoist fellowship manifests a serene freedom which matches Chuang-tzu's description of the "Man of Spirit, the Nameless One." He can only be identified as Muriel's father's uncle, a tiny deaf-mute, whose silent composure underscores the tumultuous distress of those around him. When we first meet him in the limousine filled with wedding guests, he is sitting next to Bunny. Unlike the Matron of Honor, however, he has plenty of room ("his silk hat cleared the roof of the car by a good four or five inches") and creates psychic space for Buddy through unaccusing silence. Diminutive, he seems unique among the suffering "grownups," especially since his stature corresponds to an egolessness that spares him anguish. Buddy, on the other hand, suffering from pleurisy and pressed into service as a doorman after the abortive ceremony ("like . . . a young giant with a cough"), bangs his head against the car roof. Miserable, he still rejoices in the nameless man's presence. "When I'd originally loaded the car, I'd a passing impulse to pick him up bodily and insert him gently through the window." Concentrated and present as none of his self-conscious companions can be, the old man resembles the Taoist ideal of the Perfect Man who "has no self." Chuang-tzu distinguishes such serenity by affirming that "great understanding is broad and unhurried; little understanding is cramped and busy. Great words are clear and limpid; little words are shrill and quarrelsome." The Nameless One embodies this opposition to unavailing distress: "Let your mind wander in simplicity, blend your spirit with the vastness, follow along with things the way they are, and make no room for personal views." And his attention certainly suggests a Taoist childlike attitude as well as Franny's own analogous receptiveness to Seymour's reading. Thus, he calmly just sits "staring very severely straight ahead of him," reminiscent of Chuang-tzu's characterization of a "childlike stare" embracing mystery as "the understanding of that which is not to be understood," namely the ineffable Tao itself. As the Nameless One, he is egolessness and silence incarnate. Mute and detached, he suggests both Kao's forgetfulness of the inessential as well as Seymour's visionary presence, a dwelling in immediate formless simplicity that transcends the dichotomy of subject and object. According to Lu Chi-p'u, "freedom from words, or *hai-yen*, means that Tao expresses itself; this is called the essence of nature. When one listens to it, nothing is heard. It is the state of namelessness and selflessness."

Salinger underscores the Nameless One's detachment when he contrasts his composure with the huge Matron of Honor's childish "little plaint of frustration and pique." "The delay didn't seem to affect him. His standard of comportment for sitting in the rear seat of cars . . . seemed to be fixed. . . . You just sat very erect . . . and you stared ferociously ahead at the windshield. . . . If Death . . . stepped miraculously through the glass and came in after you, in all probability you just got up and went along with him." Such detachment echoes Chuang-tzu's prescription for living in the Tao: "being upright, you will be still; being still, you will be enlightened; being enlightened, you will be empty; and being empty, you will do nothing, and yet there will be nothing that is not done." The Nameless One's inaction conforms to Chuang-tzu's teaching: "the inaction of heaven is its purity, the inaction of earth is its peace." Calmly facing death, he resembles the Taoist ideal of the child who "stares all day without blinking its eyes—it has no preferences in the world of externals."

Nameless, useless, simply himself, he transcends classification, yet he alone among the wedding guests communicates without acrimony or pretense. A single written word of acceptance, "Delighted," expresses his whole being in an act of *disponibilité* that affirms the underlying Taoist perspective. Chuang-tzu urges liberation from worldly concerns because conventional values impede this mystical freedom and keep one shackled. Hence, if one wishes freedom, one must practice wu-wei which creates harmony by letting all human actions "become as spontaneous as those of the natural world." And Taoism values such childlike immediacy and nonconflictual action because the self, once empty of egocentric striving, has no need to compete. Like Kao or the superlative horse, the Nameless One interacts harmoniously with the universe and leaves no trace: being emptiness itself, he creates space for all.

According to Chuang-tzu, this emptiness necessitates "fasting of the heart," whose goal is inner unity:

> This means . . . hearing with the spirit, with your whole being . . . [which] is not limited to any one faculty, to the ear, or to the mind. Hence it demands the emptiness of all the faculties. . . . Then the whole being listens. There is then a direct grasp of what is right there before you that can never be heard with the ear or understood with the mind. Fasting of the heart . . . frees you from limitation and from preoccupation . . . and begets unity and freedom.
>
> Look at this window: . . . because of it the whole room is full of light. So when the faculties are empty, the heart . . . full of light . . . becomes an influence by which others are secretly transformed.

Thus centered and empty in the Taoist sense, the nameless old man, like Kao, is appropriately cut off from the inessential. Salinger symbolically indicates this "fasting of the heart" by depriving him of speech, hearing, and preferences. Death and life, movement and immobility, solitude and companionship, are alike to him because he, like Lieh-tzu, rests in the emptiness of wu-wei. And this immersion in the Tao's simplicity makes him a window and a refuge that secretly transforms Buddy.

Salinger emphasizes the old man's divine quality through Buddy's drunken questions. "Don't you have a home to go to? Who looks after you? The pigeons in the Park?" Such radical homelessness, unconditional dependence upon God's care, and joyful lack of self-concern ("in response to these provocative questions, my host toasted me with renewed gusto") recall the gospel passages about the blessed freedom of the Beatitudes, the lilies of the fields, and the Son of Man having no place to rest his head. Yet here again Salinger's religious pluralism makes us aware of further ranges of meaning within this image of homelessness. Indeed, this wandering pilgrim suggests not only the Taoist Nameless One and

the biblical and liturgical theme of the people of God journeying toward the
the heavenly Jerusalem: he also alludes to the ancient Indian ideal of *sannyāsa*,
homeless existence as a wandering mendicant, the final stage of traditional
Hindu ascesis. As a type of sannyāsi, he practices self-denial characteristic of one
who has abandoned all human security and certitude and now searches for the
infinite. Ministering to Buddy's need, he manifests the Hindu values of *ahiṁsā*
(nonviolence) and *brahma-carya* (quest for God), as well as the Buddhist perfection of *karuṇā* (compassion), *maitri* (loving kindness), *prājña* (wisdom), and
śūnyatā (emptiness). Moreover, his self-surrender suggests Christ's own *kenosis*,
the total self-emptying to save humankind.

The old man's spiritual nature suggests his essential relation to Seymour.
This spiritual kinship appears when Buddy, anxious lest he be recognized as
Seymour's brother, glances at his friend and notices "almost with gratitude . . .
that his feet didn't quite touch the floor. They looked like old and valued friends
of mine." Salinger further strengthens this connection when Buddy lyingly tells
Bunny that Seymour "was a chiropodist," denoting a person who treats both
hands and feet, organs of special significance for Seymour. One immediately
thinks of Sybil and Seymour's feet in "A Perfect Day for Bananafish"; Charlotte
Mayhew's expressing pleasure over Seymour's performance during the radio
show by tramping on his feet ("He loved people who stepped on his feet"); and
the discussion in "Seymour" of Seymour's hands in relation to his being a Jew.
Throughout these fictions, hands and feet function as synecdoches indicating a
person's psychic state. This synecdoche figures in Seymour's diary when Mrs.
Fedder wants him to undergo analysis after he marries Muriel. "If or when, I do
start going to an analyst, I hope to God he has the foresight to let a dermatologist sit in on consultation. *A hand specialist.* I have scars on my hands from
touching certain people." These scars witness his extraordinary openness, his
refusal to exclude anyone from his life, even as the nameless one's concentrated
silence and childlike availability reveal a whole-hearted participation in the *Tao*.

The old man's kinship with Seymour becomes comically clear when Buddy
hysterically denounces Bunny for attacking his brother. Reporting Mrs. Fedder's
slur "that this Seymour . . . was a latent homosexual" and "a really schizoid
personality," she then accuses him of "having never *grown up*" and of acting like
"an absolute raving maniac of some crazy kind." Buddy's reaction is understandably, but absurdly, intemperate: "I said I didn't give a good God damn what
Mrs. Fedder . . . or any professional dilettante or amateur bitch had to say. . . . I
said that not one God-damn person . . . had ever seen him for what he really
was. A poet, for God's sake. And I mean a *poet.* If he never wrote a line of
poetry, he could still flash what he had at you with the back of his ear if he
wanted to." The only thing that stopped Buddy's self-indulgent attack was the
sound of the toilet being flushed by the nameless old man. Now given this

bizarre wedding reception, we probably should not be surprised to find a shouting match between the matron of honor and the surrogate groom that ends with a toilet being flushed by a nameless deaf-mute. His nonverbal contribution to a parodic epithalamion seems ironically appropriate, especially since Buddy describes his speech as "the polluted stream of invective I'd loosed on them." Besides the scatological humor reminiscent of Chaucer and the chapel scene in *The Catcher in the Rye*, the Nameless One's spontaneous offering has a deeper significance. Buddy's harangue about Seymour's not being recognized as a poet recalls his earlier response to the old man's "Delighted," when, as he says, "I . . . tried to show by my expression that all of us in the car knew a poem when we saw one." "The universally familiar sound of plumbing," the old man's comic "poem," identifies him with Seymour, whose transcendent poetry did not rely on words either.

In harmony with the Taoist teaching that the Heavenly Way is just as much present in excrement as it is in the most sublime human experiences, the old man's poem prompts Buddy to let go his anger and judgmentalism. As such, it recalls Chuang-tzu's invitation to accompany him to "the palace of Nowhere where all the many things are One." The "palace of Nowhere" in "the land of Non-Doing" suggests Zooey's intuition of wu-wei, where indeed "all the many things are One." This confluence of all living things in turn evokes Eliot's "still-point of the turning world" and the eschatological vision of the messianic banquet, where all creation shall find nourishment and rest.

III

Rather than blurring or collapsing different Oriental and Western traditions, Salinger's religious pluralism finds artistic expression in a respectful and playful interraction of distinct layers of meaning. This playful respect, which distinguishes his aesthetic and relates it to Taoist and Buddhist practice, appears in his customary use of simple words and images to convey complex themes. The ending of "Raise High" is a case in point. Waking to find the old man gone, Buddy concludes that only "his empty glass, and cigar end in the pewter ashtray, indicated that he had ever existed. I still rather think his cigar end should have been forwarded on to Seymour, the usual run of wedding gifts being what it is. Just the cigar in a small, nice box. Possibly with a blank sheet of paper enclosed, by way of explanation." In this final part of my argument, I will demonstrate how these three objects—the glass, cigar, and sheet of paper "by way of explanation"—reveal Salinger's aesthetic and the story's pattern of densely woven religious meaning. But before attempting these interconnections, we must examine the objects individually.

The empty glass has an extraordinary polysemous richness. Symbolizing egolessness and self-transcendence, it establishes the final link between the Name-less One and Seymour Glass. Like the ecstatic Seymour, the old man (also a poet) has gone beyond ordinary human modes of hearing, understanding, and presence. So like Lao-tzu disappearing into the West, Lieh-tzu riding the wind, Kao immersing himself in the vision of spiritual things, and Mi Yu-jen floating "up and down with the sky," he abandons everything in simple detachment. Thus, in harmony with Chuang-tzu's "fasting of the heart," his empty glass functions as a clear window clarifying Salinger's meaning through a metaphor of the mind and heart disciplined, still, and "full of light." This metaphor further suggests the "emptiness" or perfect freedom of the human faculties now resting in Tao.

Besides indicating the spiritual qualities common to these two poets, the glass also stands as a synecdoche of their paradoxical space-time presence in the story. The bridegroom, for example, never appears but his absence dominates the entire day. Indeed, his fatal "retirement" from the scene apparently colors Buddy's art and oppresses his very being. This powerful absence moves us for-ward and backward through time as Salinger's allusively structured narrative shuttles us between 1934 (Franny hears Seymour read Lieh-tzu), 1942 (the wedding day), 1948 (Seymour's suicide), and 1955 (Buddy's puzzling through these events). But if Seymour's absence proves curiously palpable, the old man's presence is about as elusive as the superlative horse. Remote from the common distress, he is egolessly cool in their inferno. Since both poets are paradoxically present and absent, the empty glass—like the absent Glass—suggests a common passing beyond into the "palace of Nowhere."

The empty glass indicating their common passing recalls Chuang-tzu's symbol of the empty boat and the freedom of living "with Tao in the land of the great Void." His description reveals the significance of these two present-absent "empty glass" poets. "If you can empty your boat," writes Chuang-tzu, "cross-ing the river of the world, no one will oppose you. . . . Whoever can free himself from achievement . . . will flow like Tao, unseen . . . like life itself with no name and no home . . . leaving no trace." The empty glass, then, in its Taoist aspects suggests an egoless transcendence of human cares and illusions.

From a Buddhist viewpoint, the empty glass offers additional riches. Whereas Chuang-tzu portrays "the heart of the wise man" as "the mirror of heaven and earth, the glass of everything," Buddhists interpret a clear mirror as a symbol of *Nirvāṇa*, the intuition of absolute undifferentiation of pure suchness (Skt. *tathātā*). The Chinese Zen Buddhist Master, Shen-hui, understands such-ness as "our original Mind of which we are conscious; yet there is neither the one who is conscious nor that of which there is consciousness." Thus the mirror (or the empty glass/absent Glass in "Raise High") signifies a mind returned to its primal clarity, released from all dualisms and ego-consciousness. Hence, the

Chinese Buddhist dictum, "the mind of a child is the mind of a Buddha," never focuses on romantic illusions of childhood innocence but directs us toward that seeing which makes us a Buddha. By abandoning adult misperception to attain enlightenment (*bodhi*), one becomes in a sense a mirror of suchness or "form-lessness." As an empty glass or mirror, we recover our Buddha-nature, that is, we awaken to the undifferentiated totality that our only true Self is.

The Buddhist viewpoint also explains Buddy's partial enlightenment and discloses a wider circle of corresponding spiritual traditions. Enlightenment occurs in the intuition of the essential "emptiness" (Skt. śūnyatā) or interdependent contingency of everything. When this vision of śūnyatā discloses one's Buddha-nature, one grasps the essential emptiness of the human ego striving to be dominant. Accordingly, when Buddy wakes from his stupor to find the old man gone, I think Salinger implies some degree of enlightenment because the glass, cigar, and blank paper are positive and negative symbols of emptiness, Nirvāṇa, and suchness. On the one hand, they embody the exhaustion of ordinary communication, pointing us toward the extinction of subject-object modes of perception and relation, while, on the other hand, they positively suggest the consequent recovery of our Buddha-nature. This primal unity resembles the Taoist state symbolized by a virgin block of wood (*p'u*) connoting "simplicity and genuineness in spirit and heart." Mencius himself alludes to this Taoist value when he claims "the great man is one who does not lose his child's heart." This "child's heart" also accords with the Christian perfection of "purity of heart," which St. Isaac of Syria, in a passage from *The Philokalia*, another favorite text of Salinger, glosses as "compassion for all beings." Finally, this circle of correspondences becomes complete when we realize that the essence of Buddha-nature is the perfect union of compassion (karuṇā) and wisdom (prājña).

The poetic and religious richness of this circle of correspondences relates the empty glass to the cigar end and the blank sheet of paper. In this context, the cigar *end* recalls the root meaning of Nirvāṇa, a putting out, an extinction of all craving (*tanha*) and ignorance (*avidyā*). Like the Buddha who attained Nirvāṇa after extinguishing the passions, the old man passes beyond all worldly fetters and in so doing recalls *Tathā-gata* (literally, "he who is thus gone"), an honorific title of the Buddha. In this passage, he leaves behind an *extinguished* cigar end, emblematic of the human condition now transcended. This cigar *end* intimates the completeness and finality of his victory. As a symbol of the old man's utter calm in the face of Death, the *cigar* also discloses some further meanings of Nirvāṇa, namely, "liberated from existence; calmed, quieted, vanishing from sight [one thinks of the "evanescent" superlative horse and Seymour himself]; eternal bliss [cf. the Nameless One's "Delighted"]; complete satisfaction or pleasure; and deliverance" (Monier-Williams' *Sanskrit-English Dictionary*).

The uselessness of this extinguished cigar is analogous to the wordless emptiness of the blank sheet of paper enclosed "by way of explanation." Its "emptiness" bespeaks the Buddhist intuition of śūnyatā, the negative side of suchness, which words can never communicate because it transcends the subject-object, knower-known dichotomies implicit in ordinary discourse. Its nonsensical blankness also signals Buddy's comic participation in the Taoist-Zen Buddhist tradition of nonrational dialogue and transcendent silence. Reaching the limits of narration and narrativity, Buddy trusts we will accompany him in a polysemous communion of implied meanings. Here, "intent on the inward qualities," we "lose sight of the external" and become Salinger's "amateur reader" who shares (in every sense) the dedication of and to the work. And as dedicated "amateur" readers, we share the silence of implied meanings which the blank paper symbolizes and completes. Explaining nothing, it directs us beyond ordinary syntactic and semantic constraints to the Nothing of śūnyatā and wu-wei. Thus, this blankness does not eliminate meaning but rather transposes it to another key, where it becomes a metaphor of and inducement to Buddha consciousness, a vehicle for provoking enlightenment. As a vehicle of enlightenment, this blank explanation both complements and refers back to the empty glass and extinguished cigar end as well as to the Taoist block of wood (p'u), the old man's namelessness, the Buddhist vision of ineffable suchness, and Seymour's "retirement" and wordless poetry. All these instances of apparent blankness, absence, and semantic transposition make sense within a pluralistic religious perspective open to the mystery of revelatory silence, which is really a form of prayer, a communion with the divine.

Faced with the complex religious pluralism which structures Salinger's Glass family chronicles, we should not expect to eliminate the mystery surrounding Seymour Glass's life and death. While thinking about these issues, I came across a comment by a twentieth-century Carthusian contemplative that seemed particularly pertinent. According to this anonymous monk of La Valsainte, a monastary high in the Swiss Alps, "All life is fraught with mystery both in its origins and in its workings. Thus the spiritual life, which is the most mysterious of all, life's very essence, is the most hidden and the least explicable; for it is too simple and too infinite, preventing words and beyond expression." Now given Salinger's immersion in spiritual questions and the congruent interests and callings of his characters (Seymour's *dharma* as a *mukta*, poet, and seer; Waker's vocation as a Carthusian; Franny and Zooey's questing after God; Buddy's attempt to be his brother's keeper), I believe the creator of the Glass family might agree with this view of religious mystery. And if this explication of "Raise High" can only take us to the edge of mystery, it should stress how much this story abides and has meaning within this mystery. We have already noted, for example, the mystical realities implied through the cigar, the empty glass, and the sheet of paper. Now, in conclusion, I will suggest how this blank paper poetically entails Seymour and Muriel's marriage bed, Buddy's relation to his brother, and Boo Boo's rash judgment of the bride.

The blank paper symbolizes the "inconclusive" narrative, the unfulfilled possibilities of the wedding celebration, and the range of suspended meanings that make this text so difficult to interpret. Of all the characters and issues in this story, the bride herself remains a total blank, a *terra incognita*. And here again Salinger returns us to the beginning, where Boo Boo describes Muriel as "a zero . . . but terrific looking. I don't actually know she's a zero." As amateur readers, we've learned that we *know* only by penetrating externals. She may come across as a "zero," but to one who is "ecstatically happy" and "sees more" than routine adult misperception allows, Muriel fully deserves his love. Yet here Salinger may be hinting that sexual passion limits Seymour's vision. The poem of Sappho which Boo Boo writes in soap on Seymour's bathroom mirror serves not only as a parodic epithalamion (it anticipates messages traditionally written on the windshield of the honeymoon couple's car), it also provides the title of Salinger's story. Thus, the poem seems significant, especially since it obscures (no matter how delightfully) Seymour's mirror and therefore seems to portend some psychic confusion. Sappho describes the bridegroom as "taller far than a tall man," which recent scholarship interprets as having appropriate ithyphallic connotations. Whether or not Muriel's extraordinary beauty and his own presumably intense sexual desire blind Seymour, it is certain that her name means "bright sea," and in his eyes she is nothing less than Aphrodite. Salinger may be ironically invoking Muriel's mythical identity when he has his hero commit suicide on a twin bed opposite his sleeping wife at a seaside resort in Florida. Accurately or not, the suicidal visionary now refers to his wife as "Miss Spiritual Tramp." Finally, one could argue that Muriel Fedder, as the daughter of Rhea, whose name recalls the Great Mother Goddess and the death and castration of her multitudinous lovers, unwittingly "fetters" Seymour, binding him to her limiting, unspiritual world.

While this negative view of Muriel as a spiritual "zero" seems initially plausible, I think Salinger's critique of adult misperception must balance any such interpretation. Boo Boo's description suggests the many senses of *śūnya*, the Sanskrit etymon for "zero," used by Buddhist metaphysicians and mystics to describe ultimate wisdom. Śūnya or śūnyatā, "emptiness," paradoxically denotes fullness, limitless presence, radical interrelatedness, and the perfectly ordinary. According to D. T. Suzuki, śūnyatā, as "zero," does not mean "a mathematical symbol. It is the infinite—a storehouse or womb (*garbha*) of all possible good or values." Thus Seymour marries Muriel, this Aphrodite-zero, and thereby embraces the Taoist life of indiscrimination, mirroring its essential formlessness, its egolessness that seems foolishness but is truly wisdom. By specifying a *sheet* of paper, rather than a piece or a *page*, Salinger directs our attention back to the marriage bed and Seymour's diary which Buddy thrusts in anger among the discarded sheets. In this sense, the blank sheet of paper may indicate Buddy's forgiveness of Seymour and his own kinship with the Nameless One. Transcending judgmental language, if only for a moment, Buddy's wordless gesture could suggest a movement toward renunciation of his anger and the related desire to control Seymour. The religious plenum which nourishes and structures this story leads me to suggest that the blank sheet of paper, which, like Indra's net, perfectly reflects every other facet of the narrative, is both comic gift and suitable memento of the wedding, the couple, and Seymour's vision: not lack, but fullness, a polysemy beyond words, an intuitive suchness which involves the sacred mysteries of sexuality, death, silence, and wisdom.

Chronology

1919	Jerome David Salinger is born in New York City on January 1, to Sol and Miriam Jillich Salinger.
1934	Enters Valley Forge Military Academy, in Pennsylvania.
1936	Graduates from Valley Forge.
1938	Travels in Europe.
1939	Attends a short story writing course taught by Whit Burnett at Columbia University. His first short story, "The Young Folks," published the following year in Whit Burnett's magazine, *Story*.
1942	Drafted into United States Army and attends Officers, First Sergeants, and Instructors School of the Signal Corps.
1943	Stationed in Nashville, Tennessee, then transferred to the Army Counter-Intelligence Corps. His short story "The Varioni Brothers" is published in the *Saturday Evening Post*.
1944	Sent to Europe, assigned to the Fourth Division of the U.S. Army, and later lands at Utah Beach as a part of the D-Day invasion force. Participates in European campaigns as Security Agent for the Twelfth Infantry Regiment.
1945–47	Discharged from Army in 1945 and begins to publish regularly in the *Saturday Evening Post*, *Esquire*, and the *New Yorker*.
1948–50	Begins long publishing relationship with the *New Yorker*. Publishes the major short stories "A Perfect Day for Bananafish," "Uncle Wiggily in Connecticut," "Just Before the War with the Eskimos," "The Laughing Man," and "For Esmé—with Love and Squalor" in the *New Yorker* during these years.

1950   The film version of "Uncle Wiggily in Connecticut," *My Foolish Heart*, is released by Samuel Goldwyn and stars Susan Hayward and Dana Andrews.

1951   *The Catcher in the Rye* published. "Pretty Mouth and Green My Eyes" published in the *New Yorker*.

1953   Moves to Cornish, New Hampshire. "Teddy" published in the *New Yorker*. *Nine Stories* published in April.

1955   Marries Claire Douglas on February 17. "Raise High the Roof Beam, Carpenters" and "Franny" are published in the *New Yorker*. A daughter, Margaret Ann, is born on December 10.

1957–59   "Zooey" and "Seymour: An Introduction" are published in the *New Yorker*.

1960   Son Matthew is born on February 13.

1961   *Franny and Zooey* published.

1963   *Raise High the Roof Beam, Carpenters* and *Seymour: An Introduction* published.

1965   "Hapworth 16, 1924" published in the *New Yorker*.

1967   Divorced.

1974   Salinger denounces the unauthorized *Complete Uncollected Short Stories of J. D. Salinger* in his only public statement in many years.

Contributors

HAROLD BLOOM, Sterling Professor of the Humanities at Yale University, is the author of *The Anxiety of Influence, Poetry and Repression*, and many other volumes of literary criticism. His forthcoming study, *Freud: Transference and Authority*, attempts a full-scale reading of all of Freud's major writings. A MacArthur Prize Fellow, he is general editor of five series of literary criticism published by Chelsea House.

WILLIAM WIEGAND teaches creative writing at San Francisco State University.

ALFRED KAZIN is Distinguished Professor of English at Hunter College, CUNY, and a member of the American Academy of Arts and Sciences. He is the author of *Contemporaries, Bright Book of Life, On Native Grounds, New York Jew*, and *An American Procession*.

DAVID D. GALLOWAY is the author of *The Absurd Hero in American Fiction* and has written other books on literature and education.

MAX F. SCHULZ is Professor of English at the University of Southern California. He is the author of *Black Humor Fiction of the Sixties: A Pluralistic Definition of Man and His World*.

HELEN WEINBERG teaches in the Literature Department at the Cleveland Institute of Art. She is the author of *The New Novel in America: The Kafkan Mode in Contemporary Fiction*.

BERNICE and SANFORD GOLDSTEIN have written, together and separately, several works on Japanese and American culture, as well as translations of Japanese authors. Sanford Goldstein is Professor of English at Purdue University.

137

GERALD ROSEN is Professor of English at Sonoma State University. He is the author of *Zen in the Art of J. D. Salinger.*

JOHN WENKE teaches English at Marquette University.

DENNIS L. O'CONNOR teaches English at George Mason University.

Bibliography

Ahrne, Marianne. "Experience and Attitude in *The Catcher in the Rye* and *Nine Stories*." *Moderna Sprach* 61 (1967): 242–63.

Alsen, Eberhard. " 'Raise High the Roof Beam, Carpenters' and the Amateur Reader." *Studies in Short Fiction* 17 (1980): 39–47.

Antico, John. "The Parody of J. D. Salinger: Esmé and the Fat Lady Exposed." *Modern Fiction Studies* 12 (1966): 325–40.

Baskett, S. S. "The Splendid/Squalid World of J. D. Salinger." *Wisconsin Studies in Contemporary Literature* 4 (1961): 48–61.

Baumbach, Jonathan. "The Saint as Young Man." *Modern Language Quarterly* 25 (1964): 461–72.

Bellman, S. I. "New Light on Seymour's Suicide: Salinger's 'Hapworth 16, 1924.' " *Studies in Short Fiction* 3 (1966): 348–51.

Bostwick, Sally. "Reality, Compassion, and Mysticism." *Midwest Review* 5 (1963): 30–43.

Bryan, James. "A Reading of Salinger's 'Teddy.' " *American Literature* 40 (1968): 352–69.

———. "The Admiral and Her Sailor in Salinger's 'Down at the Dinghy.' " *Studies in Short Fiction* 17 (1980): 174–78.

Carpenter, F. I. "The Adolescent in American Fiction." *English Journal* 46 (1957): 313–19.

Coles, Robert. "A Reconsideration of J. D. Salinger." *The New Republic* 168, 28 April 1973, 30–32.

Costello, Patrick. "Salinger and 'Honest Iago.' " *Renascence* 16 (1964): 171–74.

Dahl, James. "What About Antolini?" *Notes on Contemporary Literature* 13 (1983): 9–10.

Davison, Richard Allan. "Salinger Criticism and 'The Laughing Man': A Case of Arrested Development." *Studies in Short Fiction* 18 (1981): 1–15.

French, Warren. "Holden's Fall." *Modern Fiction Studies* 10 (1964–65): 389.

———. "Salinger's Seymour: Another Autopsy." *College English* 26 (1963): 563.

Glazier, Lyle. "The Glass Family Saga: Argument and Epiphany." *College English* 27 (1965): 248–51.

Goldstein, Bernice, and Sanford Goldstein. "Ego and 'Hapworth 16, 1924.' " *Renascence* 24 (1972): 159–67.

————. " 'Seymour: An Introduction': Writing as Discovery." *Studies in Short Fiction* 7 (1970): 248–56.

Gross, T. L. "J. D. Salinger: Suicide and Survival in the Modern World." *The South Atlantic Quarterly* 68 (1969): 452–62.

Grunwald, H. A. " 'He Touches Something Deep within Us.' " *Horizon* 4 (1962): 100–107.

Hagopian, J. V. " 'Pretty Mouth and Green My Eyes': Salinger's Paola and Francesca in New York." *Modern Fiction Studies* 12 (1966): 349–54.

Hassan, Ihab. "Almost the Voice of Silence: The Later Novelettes of J. D. Salinger." *Wisconsin Studies in Contemporary Literature* 4 (1963): 5–20.

Hinckle, Warren, et al. "A Symposium on J. D. Salinger." *Ramparts* 1 (1962): 47–66.

Howell, J. M. "Salinger in the Waste Land." *Modern Fiction Studies* 12 (1966): 367–75.

Johnson, J. W. "The Adolescent Hero: A Trend in Modern Fiction." *Twentieth Century Literature* 5 (1957): 3–11.

Kegel, C. H. "Incommunicability in Salinger's *The Catcher in the Rye*." *Western Humanities Review* 11 (1957): 188–90.

Kirschner, Paul. "Salinger and His Society: The Pattern of *Nine Stories*." *London Review* 6 (1969): 34–54.

Lane, Gary. "Seymour's Suicide Again: A New Reading of J. D. Salinger's 'A Perfect Day for Bananafish.' " *Studies in Short Fiction* 10 (1973): 27–33.

McCarthy, Mary. "J. D. Salinger's Closed Circuit." *Harper's Magazine* 225, no. 1349 (October 1962): 46–48.

McIntyre, J. P. "A Preface for *Franny and Zooey*." *Critic* 29 (1962): 25–28.

Marple, Anne. "Salinger's Oasis of Innocence." *The New Republic* 145, 18 September 1961, 22–23.

Metcalf, Frank. "The Suicide of Salinger's Seymour Glass." *Studies in Short Fiction* 9 (1972): 243–46.

O'Hara, J. D. "No Catcher in the Rye." *Modern Fiction Studies* 9 (1963–64): 370–76.

Oldsey, Bernard. "Salinger and Golding: Resurrection or Repose." *College Literature* 6 (1979): 136–44.

Phillips, Paul. "Salinger's *Franny and Zooey*." *Mainstream* 15 (1969): 32–39.

Russell, John. "Salinger's Feat." *Modern Fiction Studies* 12 (1966): 299–311.

Seitzman, Daniel. "Salinger's 'Franny': Homoerotic Imagery." *American Imago* 22 (1965): 57–76.

Seng, D. J. "The Fallen Idol: The Immature World of Holden Caulfield." *College English* 23 (1961): 203–9.

Stein, W. B. "Salinger's 'Teddy': Tat Tvam Asi or That Thou Art." *Arizona Quarterly* 29 (1974): 253–65.

Stone, Edward. "Salinger's Carrousel." *Modern Fiction Studies* 13 (1967): 520–23.

Tierce, Mike. "Salinger's 'De Daumier-Smith's Blue Period.' " *The Explicator* 42, no. 1 (1983): 56–58.

Updike, John. "Anxious Days for the Glass Family." *The New York Times*, 17 Sept. 1961.

Wiebe, D. E. "Salinger's 'A Perfect Day for Bananafish.' " *The Explicator* 23, no. 1 (1964): item 3.

Wiegand, William. "The Knighthood of J. D. Salinger." *The New Republic* 141, 19 October 1959: 19–21.

Acknowledgments

"J. D. Salinger: Seventy-Eight Bananas" by William Wiegand from *Chicago Review* 11, no. 4 (Winter 1958), © 1958 by the *Chicago Review*. Reprinted by permission.

"J. D. Salinger: Everybody's Favorite" by Alfred Kazin from *Atlantic Monthly* 208, no. 2 (August 1961), © 1961 by Alfred Kazin. Reprinted by permission of the author.

"The Love Ethic" by David D. Galloway from *The Absurd Hero in American Fiction* by David D. Galloway, © 1966 by David D. Galloway. Reprinted by permission of the author and the University of Texas Press.

"Epilogue to 'Seymour: An Introduction': Salinger and the Crisis of Consciousness" by Max F. Shulz from *Studies in Short Fiction 5*, no. 2 (Winter 1968), © 1967 by Newberry College. Reprinted by permission.

"J. D. Salinger's Holden and Seymour and the Spiritual Activist Hero" by Helen Weinberg from *The New Novel in America: The Kafkan Mode in Contemporary Fiction* by Helen Weinberg, © 1970 by Cornell University. Reprinted by permission of Cornell University Press.

"Zen and *Nine Stories*" by Bernice Goldstein and Sanford Goldstein from *Renascence: Essays on Values in Literature* 22, no. 4 (Summer 1970), © 1970 by the Catholic Renascence Society, Inc. Reprinted by permission.

"A Retrospective Look at *The Catcher in the Rye*" by Gerald Rosen from *American Quarterly* 29, no. 5 (Winter 1977), © 1977 by Gerald Rosen. Reprinted by permission of the author and *American Quarterly*.

"Sergeant X, Esmé, and the Meaning of Words" by John Wenke from *Studies in Short Fiction* 18, no. 3 (Summer 1981), © 1981 by Newberry College. Reprinted by permission.

"J. D. Salinger's Religious Pluralism: The Example of 'Raise High the Roof Beam, Carpenters' " by Dennis L. O'Connor from *The Southern Review* 20, no. 2 (April 1984), © 1984 by Dennis L. O'Connor. Reprinted by permission. The notes have been omitted.

Index

Van Gogh, Vincent, 49, 73
"Varioni Brothers, The," 29

Wakefield, Dan, 38
Waste Land, The (Eliot), 88
Werther (*Sufferings of Young Werther*), 16–17
Whitman, Walt, 119
Wordsworth, William, 55, 56

"Zooey," 6, 12, 13, 19, 21, 39, 40, 68; Buddy's role in, 15, 21, 26, 44, 45, 46; Franny Glass's role in, 26, 48, 50, 60; plot of, 23–24, 43–48; Seymour Glass's role in, 44, 46, 47, 48; Zooey Glass's role in, 14–15, 26, 27, 30, 41, 43–48

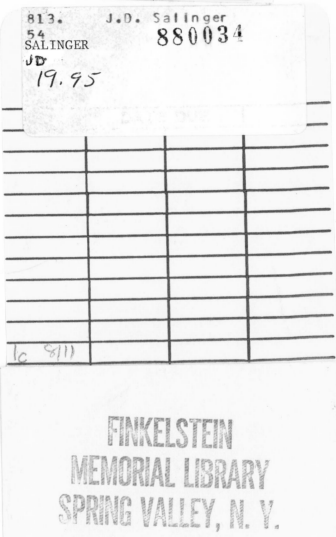